# O. HENRY

**Perfection Learning®**

**Contributing Writers:** Wim Coleman and Pat Perrin
**Editorial Director:** Susan C. Thies
**Editor:** Paula J. Reece
**Cover Art:** photos.com
**Book Design:** Emily Adickes
**Inside Illustrations:** Greg Hargreaves

© 2014 Perfection Learning®

Please visit our Web site at:
www.perfectionlearning.com

When ordering this book, please specify:
Softcover: ISBN 978-0-7891-5710-2 or **3860501**
Reinforced Library Binding: ISBN 978-0-7569-0845-4 or **3860502**
ebook: ISBN 978-0-7891-8851-9 or **38605D**

5  6  7  8  PP  18  17  16  15

Printed in the United States of America

# TABLE OF CONTENTS

# O. HENRY

O. Henry was as colorful as the characters in his stories. He was born William Sidney Porter. Showing a streak of mischief, however, he sometimes spelled his middle name Sydney, just to cause confusion. He also told people he was born in 1867 instead of 1862.

## Early Life

Young Will began working in his uncle's pharmacy at the age of ten, eventually becoming a licensed pharmacist. It was at the pharmacy that he first found his artistic talent, not as a writer, but as an illustrator. He drew sketches of the men who loitered at the counter, his illustrations then finding their way to the local newspaper. His love of words also began to show at this time. When asked his favorite book, Will would answer, "the dictionary." Friends often found him reading the dictionary for fun, and this habit lasted throughout his lifetime.

## Prison Sentence

When he was 20, Will moved to Texas and began working as a banker. He also started writing stories. After getting married and having a baby daughter, Will learned he was being investigated for embezzlement from the bank where he worked. He denied that he took any money, but he was convicted and sentenced to five years in prison.

He continued to write in prison, always using different pen names, to cover the shame of being a convicted felon. After three years he was released for good behavior. When Will left the jailhouse, out stepped O. Henry. That name became his identity as a writer from then on.

## Famous Writer

O. Henry's writing career took off after he moved to New York City. Before his death in 1910, he published over 300 more stories and became America's favorite short story writer.

In 1918 O. Henry's legacy was strengthened when the O. Henry Awards for magazine stories were established. They continue to be given each year.

# RETOLD UPDATE

This book presents a collection of eight adapted stories from the beloved American author, O. Henry. The collection represents O. Henry's range of characters, often glorifying the less accepted side of society while maintaining the irony of his story lines and the humor in his voice. The minute details of the original stories are here, but longer sentences and paragraphs in the stories have been split up. Some old or difficult words, which O. Henry particularly favored, have been replaced with easier, more modern language.

In addition, a word list has been added at the beginning of each story to make reading easier. Each word defined on that list is printed in dark type within the story. If you forget a word while you're reading, just check the list to review the definition.

You'll also see footnotes at the bottom of some story pages. These notes identify people or places, define colloquial or outdated terms, explain ideas, or even let you in on a joke.

Finally, at the end of each tale, you'll find additional information relating to the story. Sometimes it will give you background on the story or O. Henry's life and the times. In other instances it will expand on literary techniques. These revealing facts will give you further insight into O. Henry's works.

This set of stories includes some of O. Henry's most popular character sketches and others that reflect his perspective on the ironies of life and the ordinary citizen.

O. Henry was an ordinary but colorful man. His life, indeed, would have made for a good O. Henry story. How ironic!

# Memoirs of a Yellow Dog

## VOCABULARY PREVIEW

Below is a list of words that appear in the story. Read the list and get to know the words before you start the story.

**anonymous**—of unknown origin; lacking distinction
**biped**—any two-footed animal
**dolefully**—with grief; sadly
**driveling**—childish and foolish; babbling
**frolicked**—played and ran about happily
**matrimonial**—relating to marriage or married persons
**pedigree**—ancestry; purity of breed
**primeval**—relating to the earliest ages; original
**profitably**—in a way that pays off
**promenading**—strolling; parading
**saffron**—moderate orange to orange-yellow
**upholstered**—furniture covered with fabric, padding, and springs to make a soft covering

# Memoirs of a Yellow Dog

*A dog named Lovey lived a life that wasn't fit for man or beast. But one day, everything changed.*

I don't suppose it will knock any of you people off your seats to read a contribution from an animal. Mr. Kipling[1] and a good many others have demonstrated the fact that animals can express themselves **profitably** in English. No magazine goes to press nowadays without an animal story in it. Only the old-style monthlies are still running pictures of Bryan[2] and of the Mount Pelee horror.[3]

But you needn't look for any stuck-up literature in my piece. You won't find anything such as Bearoo, the bear, and Snakoo, the snake, and Tammanoo, the tiger. There's no talk here like in those jungle books.

I'm just a yellow dog who spent most of his life in a cheap New York flat.[4] I sleep in a corner on an old satin underskirt. (It's the one my owner spilled wine on at the Lady Longshoremen's[5] banquet). So I shouldn't be expected to perform any fancy tricks with the art of speech.

I was born a yellow pup—date, location, **pedigree**, and weight unknown. The first thing I can recall, an old woman had me in a basket at Broadway and Twenty-third. She was trying

---

1   Rudyard Kipling (1865–1936) was an English author of novels, short stories, and poetry. His best-known works for children—*The Jungle Book* and *The Second Jungle Book*—feature talking animals.

2   William Jennings Bryan (1860–1925) was a famous speaker who ran unsuccessfully for president in 1896, 1900, and 1908.

3   Mount Pelee is a volcano in the West Indies. In 1902, lava burst through the side of the mountain and destroyed several plantations and a town.

4   A *flat* is an apartment that is on one floor of a building.

5   A *longshoreman* is a dock worker who loads and unloads ships.

to sell me to a fat lady. Old Mother Hubbard[6] was advertising me as a genuine Pomeranian-Hambletonian-Red-Irish-Cochin-China-Stoke Poges fox terrier.[7]

The fat lady chased a five-dollar bill around among the fabric samples in her shopping bag till she cornered it and it gave up. She handed it to the old woman. From that moment I was a pet—a "mamma's own wootsey quidlums."

Say, gentle reader, did you ever have a 200-pound woman breathing a flavor of Camembert[8] and Peau d'Espagne[9] pick you up? Did she ever rub her nose all over you? Did she remark all the time in an Emma Eames[10] tone of voice, "Oh, oo's um oodlum, doodlum, woodlum, toodlum, bitsy-witsy skoodlums?"

From pedigreed yellow pup I grew up to be an **anonymous** yellow mongrel. I looked like a cross between an Angora cat and a box of lemons. But my mistress never caught on.

She thought that the two **primeval** pups that Noah chased into the ark were just a supporting branch of my ancestors. It took two policemen to keep her from entering me in a dog show at the Madison Square Garden[11] for the Siberian bloodhound prize.

I'll tell you about that flat. It was in a typical New York house. The house was paved with Parian marble in the entrance hall and cobblestones above the first floor.[12] Our flat was three—well, not flights—climbs up. My mistress rented it unfurnished. She put in the regular things—1903 antique **upholstered** parlor furniture, oil painting of geishas[13] in a Harlem tea house, rubber plant, and husband

---

6    Old Mother Hubbard is a character who has a dog in a children's nursery rhyme.
7    These are names of horse, chicken, and pig breeds as well as dog breeds. Stoke Poges is a fashionable residential district in Buckinghamshire, England; fox terrier dogs were developed in England.
8    Camembert is a soft French cheese.
9    "Peau d'Espagne" pokes fun at the names of perfumes, such as "Eau d'Paris."
10   Emma Eames (1865–1952) was a famous singer admired for her expressive voice.
11   Madison Square Garden is a sports arena in New York City where important dog shows were held.
12   Paria is an island that was famous for its fine marble in ancient times. *Cobblestones* are paving stones used on streets.
13   *Geishas* are women in Japan who are highly trained in conversation, dancing, singing, and social skills.

By Sirius![14] That was a **biped** I felt sorry for. He was a little man with sandy hair and whiskers a good deal like mine. Henpecked?[15] Well, toucans and flamingos and pelicans[16] all had their bills in him.

The husband wiped the dishes and listened to my mistress talk. She'd describe the cheap, ragged things the lady with the squirrel-skin coat on the second floor hung out on her line to dry. And every evening while she was getting supper, she made him take me out on the end of a string for a walk.

If men knew how women pass the time when they are alone, they'd never marry. Reading Laura Jean Jibbey,[17] eating peanut brittle, rubbing a little almond cream on the neck muscles, leaving the dishes unwashed. Talking for half an hour with the iceman, reading a package of old letters, downing a couple of pickles and two bottles of beer. Spending one hour peeking through a hole in the window shade into the flat across the air shaft.[18] That's about all there is to it.

Twenty minutes before it's time for him to come home from work, she straightens up the house. She fixes her rat[19] so it won't show and gets a lot of sewing done for a ten-minute bluff.

I led a dog's life in that flat. Most all day I lay there in my corner watching that fat woman kill time. I slept sometimes and had pipe dreams.[20] I dreamed about being out chasing cats into basements and growling at old ladies with black mittens. That's what a dog was intended to do.

Then she would pounce upon me with a lot of that **driveling** poodle talk. She'd kiss me on the nose—but what could I do? A dog can't chew garlic.

I began to feel sorry for Hubby. We looked so much alike that people noticed it when we went out. So we got away from

---

14 Sirius, in the constellation Canis Major, is the brightest star in the sky. It is also called the Dog Star.

15 *Henpecked* refers to a husband who is constantly controlled and nagged by his wife.

16 Toucans, flamingos, and pelicans are all birds with large beaks.

17 Laura Jean Libbey was a writer of romance novels.

18 An *air shaft* is a vertical opening through the floors of a building. It provides air and some light to inside windows.

19 A *rat* is a pad of hair or other material worn to puff out a woman's own hair.

20 A *pipe dream* is a fantasy, a dream, or plan of something that isn't likely to happen.

the streets that Morgan's[21] cab drives down. We took to climbing the piles of last December's snow on the streets where cheap people live.

One evening we were **promenading** in this way, and I was trying to look like a prize St. Bernard. The old man was trying to look like he wouldn't have murdered the first organ-grinder[22] he heard playing the wedding march. I looked up at him and said, in my way, "What are you looking so sour about, you stuffed lobster? She don't kiss you. You don't have to sit on her lap and listen to her talk. You ought to be thankful you're not a dog. Brace up, Benedick,[23] and bid the blues begone."

The **matrimonial** mishap looked down at me with almost canine intelligence in his face. "Why, doggie," he said, "good doggie. You almost look like you could speak. What is it, doggie—cats?"

Cats!

But, of course, he couldn't understand. Humans don't understand the speech of animals. The only place where dogs and men can communicate is in fiction.

In the flat across the hall from us lived a lady with a black-and-tan terrier. Her husband strung it and took it out every evening. But he always came home cheerful and whistling. One day I touched noses with the black-and-tan in the hall, and I asked him for an explanation.

"See here, Wiggle-and-Skip," I said. "You know that it ain't the nature of a real man to play nanny to a dog in public. I never saw one leashed to a bow-wow yet that didn't look like he'd like to lick every other man that looked at him. But your boss comes in every day as perky and confident as an amateur magician doing the egg trick. How does he do it? Don't tell me he likes it."

"Him?" said the black-and-tan. "Why, he uses Nature's Own Remedy. He gets drunk. By the time we've been in eight saloons, he don't care whether the thing on the end of his line is a dog or a catfish. I've lost two inches of my tail trying to

---

21  John Pierpont Morgan (1837–1913) was a wealthy and well-known financier.

22  An *organ-grinder* is a street musician who operates a hand organ.

23  In Shakespeare's play *Much Ado About Nothing,* Benedick is the young lord of Padua, known for his dislike of women.

sidestep those swinging doors."

The pointer I got from that terrier got me thinking.

One evening about 6 o'clock my mistress ordered the old man to get busy and take Lovey out. I have concealed it until now, but that is what she called me. The black-and-tan was called "Tweetness." I consider that I have one up on him. Still, being called "Lovey" is something of a tin can on the tail of one's self-respect.

At a quiet place on a safe street, I tightened the line of the old man in front of an attractive, refined saloon. I made a dead-ahead scramble for the doors, whining like a dog in the news stories—the one that lets the family know that little Alice is drowning while gathering lilies in the brook.

"Why, darn my eyes," says the old man, with a grin. "Darn my eyes if the **saffron**-colored son of a seltzer lemonade ain't asking me in to take a drink. Lemme see—how long's it been? I believe I'll—"

I knew I had him. He sat at a table and drank Hot Scotches. For an hour he kept the drinks coming. I sat by his side rapping for the waiter with my tail and eating free lunch. The food was such as mamma in her flat never equalled—her "homemade" food bought at a delicatessen eight minutes before papa comes home.

Soon the products of Scotland were all consumed except the rye bread. Then the old man unwound me from the table leg. Once outside, he took off my collar and threw it into the street, just as a fisherman throws a salmon back into the river.

"Poor doggie," he said. "Good doggie. She won't kiss you anymore. It's a darned shame. Good doggie, go away and get run over by a streetcar and be happy."

But I refused to leave. I leaped and frisked around the old man's legs, happy as a pug on a rug.[24]

"You old flea-headed woodchuck chaser," I said to him. "You moon-baying, rabbit-pointing, egg-stealing old beagle. Can't you see that I don't want to leave you? Can't you see that it's us against her? She's after you with the dish towel and me with the flea powder and a pink bow to tie on my tail. Why not

---

24  This is a takeoff on the saying, "Happy as a bug in a rug." A *pug* is a breed of dog.

cut that all out and be partners forever more?"

Maybe you'll say he didn't understand—maybe he didn't. But he kind of got a grip on the Hot Scotches and stood still for a minute, thinking.

"Doggie," he said finally, "we don't live more than a dozen lives on this earth. And very few of us live to be more than 300. If I ever see that flat anymore, I'm a flat. And if you do, you're flatter—and that's no flattery. I'm betting 60 to 1 that Westward Ho wins out by the length of a dachshund."[25]

There was no string, but I **frolicked** along with my master to the Twenty-third Street ferry. And the cats on the route saw reason to give thanks that they were born with claws.

When we reached Jersey, my master said to a stranger who stood eating a pastry, "Me and my doggie, we are bound for the Rocky Mountains."

But what pleased me most was when my old man pulled both of my ears until I howled. He said, "You common, monkey-headed, rat-tailed, yellow-colored son of a doormat, do you know what I'm going to call you?"

I thought of "Lovey," and I whined **dolefully**.

"I'm going to call you 'Pete,' " said my master. And if I'd had five tails I couldn't have done enough wagging to do justice to the occasion.

---

25  The old man means that they are going to leave for the West. A *dachshund* is a breed of dog that is long and skinny.

## INSIGHTS

"Mr. Kipling and a good many others have demonstrated the fact that animals can express themselves profitably in English," says the dog narrator at the beginning of "Memoirs of a Yellow Dog." Rudyard Kipling's *The Jungle Book,* with its many talking animals, had been published several years before this story.

But O. Henry was also probably thinking of another popular animal story when he wrote this piece. In 1903, Jack London's novel *The Call of the Wild* had been published and was a huge success. It tells the story of a dog named Buck. Buck starts off as a pet in California and winds up the leader of a wolf pack in the distant north.

London wrote other stories with dog characters, including the novel *White Fang* and the short story "Brown Wolf" (included in *Retold Jack London).* London's dog characters frequently have to choose between loyalty to their masters and the lure of the wilderness.

"Memoirs of a Yellow Dog" cleverly turns the tables on London. In O. Henry's story, the dog never considers leaving his master. His master, on the other hand, makes a run for the wilderness to escape married life.

# The Ransom of Red Chief

## VOCABULARY PREVIEW

Below is a list of words that appear in the story. Read the list and get to know the words before you start the story.

**aimlessly**—without aim or purpose

**anxiously**—with worry and fear

**captive**—prisoner

**chronic**—lasting a long time

**desperate**—having lost hope

**egotism**—the habit of being too self-centered or proud of oneself

**ferocious**—fierce and cruel

**imp**—child who enjoys making mischief

**impudent**—rude and sassy

**porous**—filled with small openings

**prominent**—leading or well-known

**proposition**—a suggested scheme

**provisions**—supplies, especially food and drink

**spendthrift**—one who foolishly and wastefully spends money

**sullenly**—in a gloomy and sulky way

**terrorized**—frightened

**treachery**—an act that betrays a person, group, or country; disloyalty

# The Ransom of Red Chief

*When two con men decide to kidnap a wild ten-year-old boy and hold him for ransom, the scheme doesn't go quite as the men had planned.*

It looked like a good thing, but wait till I tell you. We were down South in Alabama—Bill Driscoll and myself—when we thought of this kidnapping idea. It was "during an instant of momentary madness," as Bill said afterward. But we didn't find that out till later.

There was a town down there as flat as a pancake. It was called Summit,[1] of course. The people who lived there were as harmless and happy a group of peasants as ever gathered around a maypole.[2]

Bill and me had about 600 dollars between us. We needed just 2,000 dollars more to pull off a dishonest scheme in western Illinois.

We talked it over on the front steps of the hotel. Parents' love for their children, say we, is strong in little towns. So a kidnapping job should do better there than in areas where reporters are sent out to stir up talk.

We knew that Summit couldn't come after us with anything stronger than the police and maybe some lazy bloodhounds. And maybe they'd write an angry line or two in the *Weekly Farmers' Budget*. So it looked good.

We chose for our victim the only child of a **prominent** citizen named Ebenezer Dorset. The father was respectable and

---

1 A *summit* is a high point in an area. The narrator is being sarcastic.

2 A *maypole* is a tall, flower-wreathed pole forming a center for May Day sports and dances.

tight with his money. He was a mortgage buyer; a stern, honest passer of collection plates; and a forecloser.[3]

The kid was a ten-year-old boy with freckles that stood out. Bill and I figured that we could shake down Ebenezer for a ransom of 2,000 dollars to the last cent. But wait till I tell you. About two miles from Summit was a little mountain covered with a thick growth of cedars. At the back of the mountain near the top was a cave. There we stored **provisions.**

One evening after sundown, we drove in a buggy past old Dorset's house. The kid was in the street. He was throwing rocks at a kitten on a fence.

"Hey, little boy!" says Bill. "Would you like to have a bag of candy and a nice ride?"

The boy hits Bill square in the eye with a piece of brick.

"That will cost the old man an extra 500," says Bill.

That boy put up a fight like a boxing bear. At last we got him down in the bottom of the buggy and drove away. We took him up to the cave. Then I hitched the horse in the cedars.

After dark I drove the buggy three miles to the little village where we had rented it. Then I walked back to the mountain.

Bill was putting bandages over the scratches and bruises on his face. There was a fire burning behind the big rock at the entrance of the cave. The boy was watching a pot of boiling coffee. He had two buzzard tail feathers stuck in his red hair.

He points a stick at me when I come up and says, "Ha, damned paleface! Do not dare to enter the camp of Red Chief, the terror of the plains!"

Bill rolled up his pants and looked at the bruises on his legs. "We're playing Indian. We're making Buffalo Bill's show seem as exciting as a town meeting.[4] I'm Old Hank, the Trapper, Red Chief's **captive.** I'm to be scalped at daybreak. By Geronimo, that kid can kick hard!"

Yes, sir, that boy seemed to be having the time of his life. The fun of camping out in a cave had made him forget that he was a captive himself. He named me Snake-Eye, the Spy. He

---

3   A *mortgage* is a deed that gives someone a claim to property in case a debt is not repaid. To *foreclose* is to take over a piece of property when a debt is not repaid.

4   Bill means that their play is so wild that it tops Buffalo Bill's Wild West Show.

told me when his braves returned from the warpath, I was to be broiled at the stake at dawn.

Then we had supper. He filled his mouth full of bacon and bread and gravy. At the same time, he began to talk. He made a speech during dinner that went something like this.

"I like this fine. I never camped out before. But I had a pet opossum once, and I was nine on my last birthday. I hate to go to school. Rats ate up 16 of Jimmy Talbot's aunt's speckled hen's eggs. Are there any real Indians in these woods? I want some more gravy. Does the trees moving make the wind blow? We had five puppies. What makes your nose so red, Hank? My father has lots of money. Are the stars hot? I whipped Ed Walker twice on Saturday. I don't like girls. You'd better not catch toads unless you use a string. Do oxen make any noise? Why are oranges round? Have you got beds to sleep on in this cave? Amos Murray has got six toes. A parrot can talk, but a monkey or a fish can't. How many does it take to make 12?"

Every few minutes he would remember that he was a pesky redskin. Then he'd pick up his stick rifle and tiptoe to the mouth of the cave. There he'd look for the scouts of the hated paleface.

Now and then he would let out a war whoop that made Old Hank the Trapper shake. That boy had Bill **terrorized** from the start.

"Red Chief," says I to the kid, "would you like to go home?"

"Aw, what for?" says he. "I don't have any fun at home. I hate to go to school. I like to camp out. You won't take me back home again, Snake-eye, will you?

"Not right away," says I. "We'll stay here in the cave awhile."

"All right!" says he. "That'll be fine. I never had such fun in all my life."

We went to bed about 11. We spread down some wide blankets and quilts and put Red Chief between us.

We weren't afraid he'd run away. He kept us awake for three hours, jumping up and reaching for his rifle. "Listen, partner!" he screeched in my ears and Bill's. He did this whenever he imagined that the crackle of a twig or the rustle of a leaf meant that outlaws were sneaking up.

At last I fell into a restless sleep. I dreamed that I had been kidnapped and chained to a tree by a **ferocious** pirate with red hair.

Just at daybreak, I was awakened by several awful screams from Bill. They weren't yells, or howls, or shouts such as you'd expect from a man. They were more like the screams of women when they see ghosts or caterpillars. It's an awful thing to hear a strong, **desperate**, fat man scream without any control in a cave at daybreak.

I jumped up to see what the matter was. Red Chief was sitting on Bill's chest with one hand tangled in Bill's hair. In the other he had the sharp knife we used for slicing bacon. He was trying very hard with great realism to scalp Bill. That was the sentence[5] that Bill had been given the evening before.

I got the knife away from the kid and made him lie down again. But, from that moment, Bill's spirit was broken. He lay down on his side of the bed. But he never closed an eye again to sleep as long as that boy was with us.

I dozed off for a while. But close to sunup, I remembered that Red Chief had said I was to be burned at the stake at dawn. I wasn't nervous or afraid. But I sat up, lit my pipe, and leaned against a rock.

"What are you getting up so soon for, Sam?" asks Bill.

"Me?" says I. "Oh, I got a kind of pain in my shoulder. I thought sitting up would rest it."

"You're a liar!" says Bill. "You're afraid. You was to be burned at sunrise, and you was afraid he'd do it. And he would too, if he could find a match.

"Ain't it awful, Sam? Do you think anybody will pay out money to get a little **imp** like that back home?"

"Sure," says I. "A rowdy kid like that is just the kind that parents love. Now, you and the Chief get up and cook breakfast. I'll go up on the top of this mountain and scout around."

I went up on the peak of the little mountain and ran my eye over the area. Over toward Summit, I expected to see the village folk. I thought they would be armed with scythes[6] and pitchforks, searching the countryside for the kidnappers.

---

5   A *sentence* is punishment, as in that imposed by a court on a convicted criminal.

6   *Scythes* are tools with curved blades used for cutting grass or grain.

But what I saw was a peaceful landscape and one man plowing with a mule. Nobody was searching the creek. No messengers dashed back and forth to tell the worried parents that there was no news. Instead, there was a sleepiness throughout that part of Alabama that lay before my eyes.

"Perhaps," says I to myself, "they haven't yet found out that the wolves have taken the little lamb from the flock. Heaven help the wolves!" says I. And I went down the mountain to breakfast.

When I got to the cave, I found Bill backed up against the side of it, breathing hard. The boy looked as though he was ready to smash him with a rock half as big as a coconut.

"He put a red-hot boiled potato down my back," explained Bill. "Then he mashed it with his foot. I smacked his ears. Have you got a gun with you, Sam?"

I took the rock away from the boy and kind of patched up the argument.

"I'll fix you," says the kid to Bill. "No man ever yet hit Red Chief who didn't get paid back. You better beware!"

After breakfast the kid takes something out of his pocket. It was a piece of leather with strings wrapped around it. He goes outside the cave unwinding it.

"What's he up to now?" says Bill, **anxiously**. "You don't think he'll run away, do you, Sam?"

"No fear of it," says I. "He don't seem to be much of a stay-at-home type. But we've got to fix up some plan about the ransom.

"There don't seem to be much excitement around Summit because he's disappeared. Maybe they haven't realized yet that he's gone. His folks may think he's spending the night with Aunt Jane or one of the neighbors.

"Anyhow, he'll be missed today. Tonight we must get a message to his father demanding the 2,000 dollars for his return."

Just then we heard a kind of war whoop. David might have shouted like this when he knocked out the champion Goliath.[7] It was a slingshot that Red Chief had pulled out of his pocket.

---

7   According to the Bible (1 Samuel:17), Goliath was a huge, young Philistine who challenged the Israelites. David accepted the challenge and killed Goliath with a rock from his slingshot.

Now he was whirling it around his head.

I dodged and heard a heavy thud and a kind of sigh from Bill. A horse makes the same sound when you take his saddle off. A rock the size of an egg had hit Bill just behind his left ear.

Bill went limp. Then he fell into the fire across the frying pan of hot dishwater. I dragged him out and poured cold water on his head for half an hour.

After a while, Bill sits up and feels behind his ear. He says, "Sam, do you know who my favorite Biblical character is?"

"Take it easy," says I. "You'll come to your senses shortly."

"King Herod,"[8] says he. "You won't go away and leave me here alone, will you, Sam?"

I went out and caught that boy. I shook him until his freckles rattled.

"If you don't behave," says I, "I'll take you straight home. Now, are you going to be good or not?"

"I was only playing a joke," says he **sullenly**. "I didn't mean to hurt Old Hank. But what did he hit me for? I'll behave, Snake-Eye, if you won't send me home. And if you'll let me play the Black Scout today."

"I don't know the game," says I. "That's for you and Mr. Bill to decide. He's your playmate for the day. I'm going away for a while on business.

"Now, you come in and make friends with him. Say you're sorry for hurting him. If you don't, you'll go home at once."

I made him and Bill shake hands. Then I took Bill aside and told him I was going to Poplar Cove. Poplar Cove was a little village three miles from the cave. I wanted to find out there what Summit was saying about the kidnapping.

Also, I thought it best to send a stern letter to old man Dorset that day. I was going to demand the ransom and order how it should be paid.

"You know, Sam," says Bill, "I've stood by you. Without blinking an eye, I faced earthquakes, fire, and flood. I stuck with you in poker games, dynamite explosions, police raids, train robberies, and cyclones.

---

8    The Bible says that King Herod (73?–4 B.C.) ordered all infant boys of Bethlehem to be murdered.

"I never lost my nerve yet till we kidnapped that two-legged rocket of a kid. He's got me going. You won't leave me long with him, will you, Sam?"

"I'll be back sometime this afternoon," says I. "You must keep the boy amused and quiet till I return. And now we'll write a letter to old Dorset."

Bill and I got paper and pencil and worked on the letter. Meanwhile, Red Chief strutted up and down with a blanket wrapped around him. He was guarding the mouth of the cave. Bill begged me tearfully to make the ransom 1,500 dollars instead of 2,000.

"I ain't trying," says he, "to say anything against the well-known love of parents for their kids.

"But we're dealing with humans. It ain't human for anybody to give up 2,000 dollars for that 40-pound chunk of freckled wildcat.

"I'm willing to take a chance asking 1,500. I'll even pay the difference."

So, to relieve Bill, I agreed. Together we wrote a letter that ran this way:

*EBENEZER DORSET, ESQ.,*[9]
*We have your boy hidden in a place far from Summit. It is useless for you or even the best detectives to try to find him. Absolutely the only terms on which you can have him back are these.*

*We demand 1,500 dollars in large bills for his return. The money is to be left at midnight tonight at the same spot and in the same box as your reply—as described below.*

*If you agree to these terms, send your answer in writing by a lone messenger tonight at 8:30. Take the road to Poplar Cove and cross Owl Creek. There you'll see three large trees about a hundred feet apart. They are close to the fence of the wheat field on the right-hand side. Go to the bottom of the fence post across from the third tree. You will find a small cardboard box.*

*The messenger will place the answer in this box and return*

---

9    *Esq.* is an abbreviation for "Esquire." This is a title of respect placed after a man's last name.

*immediately to Summit.*

*If you try any* **treachery** *or do not meet the demands in this letter, you will never see your boy again.*

*If you pay the money as demanded, he will be returned to you safe and well within three hours. These terms are final. If you do not agree with them, we won't try to reach you again.*

*TWO DESPERATE MEN*

I addressed this letter to Dorset. Then I put it in my pocket. As I was about to start, the kid comes up to me and says, "Aw, Snake-Eye, you said I could play the Black Scout while you was gone."

"Play it, of course," says I. "Mr. Bill will play with you. What kind of game is it?"

"I'm the Black Scout," says Red Chief. "I have to ride to the fort to warn the settlers that the Indians are coming. I'm tired of playing Indian myself. I want to be the Black Scout."

"All right," says I. "It sounds harmless to me. I guess Mr. Bill will help you outsmart the pesky Indians."

"What am I supposed to do?" says Bill, looking at the kid with suspicion.

"You are the horse," says Black Scout. "Get down on your hands and knees. How can I ride to the fort without a horse?"

"You'd better keep him interested," says I, "till we get the scheme going. Loosen up."

Bill gets down on all fours. A look comes in his eye like a rabbit's when you catch it in a trap.

"How far is it to the fort, kid?" he asks in a hoarse voice.

"Ninety miles," says the Black Scout. "And you have to move it to get there on time. Whoa, now!"

The Black Scout jumps on Bill's back. Then he digs his heels in Bill's side.

"For heaven's sake," says Bill, "hurry back, Sam, as soon as you can. I wish we hadn't made the ransom more than a thousand. Say, you quit kicking me, or I'll get up and spank you good."

I walked over to Poplar Cove and sat around the post office and store. I talked with the hicks that came in to buy something. One bearded fellow says that he hears Summit is all upset because Old Ebenezer Dorset's boy was lost or stolen.

That was all I wanted to know. I bought some smoking tobacco and casually mentioned the price of black-eyed peas. Then I secretly mailed my letter and walked away. The postmaster said the mailman would come by in an hour to take the mail to Summit.

When I got back to the cave, Bill and the boy weren't there. I searched around the cave and risked a shout or two, but there was no response.

So I lighted my pipe and sat down on a mossy bank to wait for something to happen.

In about a half an hour, I heard the bushes rustle. Bill wobbled out into the little clearing in front of the cave. Behind him was the kid. He came stepping softly like a scout, with a broad grin on his face.

Bill stopped, took off his hat, and wiped his face with a red handkerchief. The kid stopped about eight feet behind him.

"Sam," says Bill, "I suppose you'll think I'm a traitor. But I couldn't help it. I'm a grown person with a man's ways and habits of defending myself. But there is a time when all types of **egotism** and control fail.

"The boy is gone. I have sent him home. All our plans are off."

"There was martyrs[10] in old times," goes on Bill. "They died rather than give up the kind of graft[11] they enjoyed. None of 'em ever was forced to suffer such inhuman tortures as I have. I tried to be faithful to our laws of pirating. But there came a limit!"

"What's the trouble, Bill?" I ask him.

"I was rode," says Bill, "the 90 miles to the fort, not one inch less. Then, when the settlers was rescued, I was given oats. Sand ain't a tasty substitute.

"Then for an hour, I tried to explain to him why there was nothin' in holes. And I also tried to tell him how a road can run both ways and what makes the grass green.

"I tell you, Sam, a human can only stand so much. I takes him by the neck of his clothes and drags him down the mountain. On

---

10  A *martyr* is a person who heroically dies for his or her beliefs.

11  *Graft* is money dishonestly taken.

the way he kicks my legs black and blue from the knees down. And I've got to have two or three bites on my hand treated.

"But he's gone," continues Bill, "gone home. I showed him the road to Summit. I also kicked him about eight feet nearer there at one kick.

"I'm sorry we lost the ransom. But it was either that or send Bill Driscoll to the madhouse."

Bill is puffing and blowing. But there is a look of peace and growing contentment on his rosy face that can't be described.

"Bill," says I, "there isn't any heart disease in your family, is there?"

"No," says Bill. "Nothing **chronic** except malaria[12] and accidents. Why?"

"Then you might turn around," says I, "and have a look behind you."

Bill turns and sees the boy. He grows pale and sits down hard on the ground. He begins to pick **aimlessly** at grass and little sticks.

For an hour I was afraid he'd gone crazy. And I told him that my scheme was to finish up the whole job at once. We would get the ransom and be off with it by midnight if old Dorset agreed to our **proposition**.

So Bill got up enough courage to give the kid a weak smile. And he promised to play the Russian in Japanese war with him when he felt better.

I had a scheme for getting that ransom without being trapped by opposing plots. Professional kidnappers should find it interesting. The tree under which the answer and the money were to be left was close to the road fence. There were big, bare fields on all sides. If a gang of police officers should be watching for anyone to come for a note, they could see him from a long way off.

But no, sirree! At 8:30, I was up in that tree. I was as well hidden as a tree toad, waiting for the messenger to arrive.

Right on time, a half-grown boy rides up the road on a bicycle. He locates the cardboard box at the foot of the fence post. Then he slips a folded piece of paper into it. After that he

---

12 *Malaria* is a disease carried by mosquitoes, which causes fevers that recur.

pedals back toward Summit.

I waited an hour and then decided no one was going to play any tricks. I slid down the tree and got the note. Then I slipped along the fence till I reached the woods. I was back at the cave in another half an hour.

I opened the note, got near the lantern, and read it to Bill. It was written with a pen in poor handwriting. The sum and total of it was this:

*TWO DESPERATE MEN,*
*I received your letter today about the ransom for the return of my son. I think your demands are a little high. So I am now making you a proposition that I believe you will accept.*

*You will bring Johnny home and pay me 250 dollars cash. I will then agree to take him off your hands.*

*You had better come at night, for the neighbors believe he is lost. I couldn't be responsible for what they would do to anybody they saw bringing him back.*

*Very Respectfully,*
*EBENEZER DORSET*

"Great pirates of Penzance!"[13] says I; "of all the **impudent**—"

But I glanced at Bill and hesitated. He had the most pleading look I ever saw on the face of a speechless or a talking animal.

"Sam," says he, "what's 250, after all? We've got the money. One more night of this kid will send me to a bed in the madhouse.

"Besides being a true gentleman, I think Mr. Dorset is a **spendthrift** for making us such a generous offer. You ain't going to pass up the chance, are you?"

"To tell you the truth, Bill," says I, "this little lamb has got on my nerves a bit too. We'll take him home and pay the ransom. Then we'll make our getaway."

We took him home that night. We got him to go by telling him that his father had bought a rifle and a pair of moccasins for him. We also said that we were going to hunt bears the next day.

It was just 12:00 when we knocked at Ebenezer's front door.

---

13   The pirates of Penzance are in a comic opera by Gilbert and Sullivan.

Right at that moment, I should have been taking the 1,500 from the box under the tree. Instead, Bill was counting out 250 dollars into Dorset's hand.

When the kid found out we were going to leave him at home, he started to howl like a pipe organ. He grabbed Bill's leg as tight as a leech. His father peeled him away bit by bit, like a **porous** plaster.

"How long can you hold him?" asks Bill.

"I'm not as strong as I used to be," says old Dorset. "But I think I can promise you ten minutes."

"Enough," says Bill. "In ten minutes I shall cross the central, southern, and middle western states and be heading for Canada."

It was dark, and Bill was fat, and I'm a good runner. But he was a good mile and a half out of Summit before I could catch up with him.

## INSIGHTS

Many of O. Henry's stories have been adapted for radio, stage, screen, and television. In fact, silent movie versions of his stories began to appear in 1909, the year before he died. Probably the first movie of an O. Henry story was a short silent called "The Sacrifice." It was based on "The Gift of the Magi," included in this book. Three of his stories were retold in *O. Henry's Full House,* a movie made in 1952. And "The Last Leaf," also in this book, was filmed in 1998.

With its clever dialogue and comic situations, "The Ransom of Red Chief" has been especially popular for adaptation. It has been played on radio, and several stage versions have been written. It has also appeared as two TV movies—one in 1975, another in 1998.

The most famous movie version of this story treats the plot very freely. In *Ruthless People* (1986), the kidnap "victim" isn't a little boy, but an annoying wife played by Bette Midler. Her wealthy husband, played by Danny DeVito, is more than happy to have her disappear, much to the kidnappers' despair.

# The Complete Life of John Hopkins

## VOCABULARY PREVIEW

Below is a list of words that appear in the story. Read the list and get to know the words before you start the story.

**avocation**—vocation; occupation
**disposition**—temperament; personality
**droningly**—in a persistently dull or unvarying tone
**earnest**—passionate; intense
**falter**—hesitate; waver
**frankly**—straightforwardly; openly
**heiress**—a woman who receives or is entitled to receive property or money after a family member's death
**inevitable**—incapable of being avoided
**irresistibly**—in a way impossible to counteract or defeat
**paradoxically**—in a contradictory manner
**pessimism**—a tendency to emphasize the unfavorable aspects of life and expect the worst possible outcome
**sprightly**—lively; spirited
**temperate**—calm; levelheaded
**wanderlust**—strong longing for or impulse toward wandering
**zealous**—energetic; passionate

# The Complete Life of John Hopkins

*John Hopkins lived the dull life of a middle-class New Yorker. But when the chance came along to really live, he seized it—if only for a few moments.*

There is a saying that no man has tasted the full flavor of life until he has known poverty, love, and war. The truth of this saying makes it agreeable to those who like their philosophy[1] simple. The three conditions offer about all there is in life worth knowing.

A shallow thinker might say that wealth should be added to the list. Not so. Let's say that a poor man finds a long-lost quarter that has slipped through a rip into his vest lining. He sounds the pleasure of life with a deeper plumb line than any millionaire can hope to cast.[2]

It seems that the wise ruler of life has thought best to drill man in these three conditions. No one may escape all three. In rural places, the terms do not mean so much. Poverty is less pinching. Love is **temperate**. War shrinks to contests about boundary lines and the neighbors' hens.

It is in the cities that our saying becomes truer and stronger. We'll leave it to a man named John Hopkins to crowd the experience into a rather small space of time.

The Hopkins flat[3] was like a thousand others. There was a rubber plant in one window. A flea-bitten terrier sat in the other,

---

1  O. Henry is referring to the *philosophy of life*, which is an overall vision of or attitude toward life and the purpose of life.

2  When crews of ships and boats measure the depths of the waters they are in, it is called *sounding*. This is done with a plumb line.

3  A *flat* is an apartment.

wondering when he was to have his day.[4]

John Hopkins was like a thousand others. He worked at 20 dollars per week in a nine-story, red-brick building at either Insurance, Buckle's Hoisting Engines, Chiropody,[5] Loans, Pulleys, Boas Renovated,[6] Waltz Guaranteed in Five Lessons, or Artificial Limbs. We cannot learn Mr. Hopkins' true **avocation** from this slight information.

Mrs. Hopkins was like a thousand others. She had a gold-filled tooth, a lazy **disposition**, and a Sunday afternoon **wanderlust**. She loved to go down to the delicatessen[7] for homemade comforts. She was crazy about department store marked-down sales. And she felt inferior to the lady in the third-floor front flat who wore genuine ostrich feathers and had two names over her bell.

She remained glued to the windowsill for long, sticky hours. She carefully avoided the bill collector. And she paid tireless attention to the noises from the dumbwaiter shaft.[8] She had all the traits of a Gotham[9] flat-dweller.

Just a bit more philosophizing, and our story will get underway.

In the Big City, large and sudden things happen. You round a corner and thrust the rib of your umbrella into the eye of your old friend from Kootenai Falls.[10] You stroll out to pluck a sweet William[11] in the park—and, lo!—bandits attack you.

Then you're taken by ambulance to the hospital. You marry your nurse, then get divorced. She squeezes you dry when you're short on money, and you stand in a breadline.[12]

---

4   According to an old saying, "Every dog has his day."
5   *Chiropody* is another word for podiatry, meaning the medical care and treatment of the human foot.
6   A *boa* is a long, fluffy scarf of fur, feathers, or delicate fabric.
7   A *delicatessen* is a store that sells ready-to-eat food products.
8   A *dumbwaiter* is a small elevator designed to carry things like clothing and food.
9   Gotham is another name for New York City.
10  Kootenai Falls is located in northwest Montana.
11  A *sweet William* is a kind of flower.
12  A *breadline* is a line of people waiting to receive free food.

Then you marry an **heiress**, take out your laundry, and pay your club dues. And all this seemingly in the wink of an eye.

You travel the streets, and a finger points to you, a handkerchief is dropped for you, or a brick is dropped upon you. The elevator cable or your bank breaks. A restaurant meal or your wife disagrees with you. Fate tosses you about like cork crumbs in wine opened by an underpaid waiter.

The City is a **sprightly** youngster. You are red paint upon its toy, and you get licked off.

After a hasty dinner, John Hopkins sat in his tight-as-a-glove flat facing the street. He sat upon a couch and gazed with satisfied eyes at a cheap, popular print of a painting called *The Storm*, tacked against the wall. Mrs. Hopkins talked **droningly** of the dinner smells from the flat across the hall. The flea-bitten terrier gave Hopkins a look of disgust and showed a man-hating tooth.

Here was neither poverty, love, nor war. But upon such bare stems, those essentials of a complete life can grow.

John Hopkins tried to add a few raisins of conversation into the tasteless dough of life.

"Putting a new elevator in at the office," he said, not mentioning who was doing so. "And the boss is letting his whiskers grow."

"You don't mean it!" commented Mrs. Hopkins.

"Mr. Whipples," continued John, "wore his new spring suit down today. I liked it fine. It's solid gray, and—" He stopped, suddenly struck by a need that made itself known to him. "I believe I'll walk down to the corner and get a five-cent cigar," he concluded.

John Hopkins got his hat. Then he picked his way down the musty halls and stairs of the apartment building.

The evening air was mild. The streets were shrill with the careless cries of children playing games controlled by mysterious rhythms and phrases. Their elders occupied doorways and steps with lazy pipe and gossip.

Lovers were on the fire escapes. **Paradoxically**, they

made no attempt to flee the mounting flames they were there to fan. The corner cigar store John Hopkins headed toward was owned by a man named Freshmayer. He looked upon the world as a terrible place.

Hopkins, unknown in the store, entered and called pleasantly for his "bunch of spinach,[13] the cheapest brand." This remark deepened Freshmayer's **pessimism**. But he set out a brand that came dangerously near to filling the order.

Hopkins bit off the end of his cigar and lighted it at the swinging gas lamp. Feeling in his pockets to make payment, he found not a penny there.

"Say, my friend," he explained **frankly**, "I've come out without any change. I'll hand you that nickel next time I pass by."

Joy rose in Freshmayer's heart. Here was proof of his belief that the world was rotten and man, a walking evil. Without a word, he rounded the end of his counter and made an **earnest** attack upon his customer. Hopkins was no man to serve as a punching bag for a gloomy tobacconist. He quickly gave Freshmayer a black eye. This paid back the gleeful kick he had received from that dealer in goods-for-cash-only.

The force of the enemy's attack drove Hopkins back to the sidewalk. There the war raged. The peaceful wooden Indian,[14] with his carved smile, was overturned. And those on the street who delighted in fighting pressed round to view the **zealous** battle.

But then came the **inevitable** cop. He was a great bother for both the attacker and attacked. John Hopkins was a peaceful citizen who liked to play word games at night in his flat. But he still had the kind of fighting spirit that comes with battle rage.

He knocked the policeman into a grocer's sidewalk display of goods. Then he gave Freshmayer a punch. This made Freshmayer briefly regret not giving a five-cent line of

---

13  By asking for a "bunch of spinach," Hopkins is suggesting that Freshmayer's cigars are not first class.

14  Cigar stores used to feature life-sized wooden sculptures of American Indians.

credit to certain customers.

Then Hopkins took spiritedly to his heels down the sidewalk. He was closely followed by the cigar dealer and the policeman, who now wore egg on his uniform.

As Hopkins ran, he became aware of a big, low, red, racing automobile that drove beside him in the street. This auto steered to the side of the sidewalk.

Then the driver motioned to Hopkins to jump into it. Hopkins did so without slowing down, falling into the turkey-red upholstered seat beside the chauffeur.[15] The big machine made a low cough. Then it flew away like an albatross[16] down the avenue into which the street emptied.

The driver of the auto sped along without a word. He was completely masked in the goggles and devil-like outfit of a chauffeur.

"Thanks a lot, old man," called Hopkins gratefully. "I guess you've got sporting blood in you, all right. You don't admire the sight of two men trying to beat one man up. In another moment, I'd have been arrested."

The chauffeur made no sign that he had heard. Hopkins shrugged a shoulder and chewed at his cigar. His teeth had clung grimly to it throughout the fight.

After ten minutes, the auto turned into the open carriage entrance of a noble mansion of brown stone. Then the auto came to a stop, and the chauffeur leaped out.

"Come quick," he said. "The lady will explain. It is the great honor you will have, monsieur.[17] Ah, that milady[18] could call upon Armand to do this thing! But, no, I am only one chauffeur."

With violent gestures, the chauffeur showed Hopkins into the house. Hopkins was led into a small but splendid visitor's room. A young, amazingly beautiful lady rose from a chair. A charming anger burned in her eyes. Her high-arched,

---

15  A *chauffeur* is a person employed to drive a motor vehicle.
16  An *albatross* is a large seabird.
17  *Monsieur* is the French word for "mister."
18  *Milady* is a form of address for a woman of fashion or noble birth.

threadlike brows were ruffled into a delicious frown.

"Milady," said the chauffeur, bowing low, "I have the honor to tell to you that I went to the house of Monsieur Long. But I found him to be not at home. As I came back, I see this gentleman in combat against—how do you say it?—greatest odds.

"He is fighting with 5, 10, 30 men," the chauffeur continued. "Policemans, even. Yes, milady, he what you call 'swatted' 1, 3, 8 policemans. Since Monsieur Long is out, I say to myself, 'This gentleman will serve milady well.' So I bring him here."

"Very well, Armand," said the lady. "You may go." She turned to Hopkins.

"I sent my chauffeur," she said, "to bring my cousin, Walter Long. There is a man in this house who has treated me with insult and abuse.

"I have complained to my aunt," the lady added. "But she laughs at me. Armand says you are brave. In these dull days, men who are both brave and chivalrous[19] are few. May I count upon your help?"

John Hopkins thrust the remains of his cigar into his coat pocket. He looked upon this winning creature and felt his first thrill of romance.

It was a knightly love. He felt no disloyalty to the flat with the flea-bitten terrier and the lady of his choice. He had married her after a picnic of the Lady Label Stickers' Union, Lodge No. 2. He had done it on a dare and a bet of new hats and chowder[20] all around with his friend Billy McManus.

This angel who was begging him to come to her rescue was too heavenly for chowder. And as for hats—golden, jeweled crowns for her!

"Say," said John Hopkins, "just show me the guy that you've got the grouch at. I've neglected my talents as a scrapper for a while, but this is my busy night."

"He is in there," said the lady, pointing to a closed door.

---

19  *Chivalry* was a code of behavior followed in medieval times by nobles and knights. It often involved pure love between knights and ladies.

20  *Chowder* is a soup made from seafood.

"Come. Are you sure that you do not **falter** or fear?"

"Me?" said John Hopkins. "Just give me one of those roses in the bunch you are wearing, will you?"

The lady gave him a red, red rose. John Hopkins kissed it and stuffed it into his vest pocket. Then he opened the door and walked into the room. It was a handsome library, softly but brightly lit. A young man was reading there.

"Books on manners is what you'll want to study," said John Hopkins abruptly. "Get up here, and I'll give you some lessons. Be rude to a lady, will you?"

The young man looked mildly surprised. Then he rose calmly, easily caught the arms of John Hopkins, and led him **irresistibly** to the front door of the house.

"Beware, Ralph Branscombe," cried the lady, who had followed. "Be careful what you do to the gallant man who has tried to protect me."

The young man shoved John Hopkins gently out the door and then closed it.

"Bess," he said calmly, "I wish you would quit reading historical novels. How in the world did that fellow get in here?"

"Armand brought him," said the young lady. "I think you are awfully mean not to let me have that St. Bernard. I sent Armand for Walter. I was so angry with you."

"Be sensible, Bess," said the young man, taking her arm. "That dog isn't safe. He has bitten two or three people around the kennels.[21] Come now, let's go tell Auntie we are in good humor again."

Arm in arm, they moved away.

John Hopkins walked to his flat. The janitor's five-year-old daughter was playing on the steps. Hopkins gave her a nice red rose and walked upstairs. Mrs. Hopkins was playing with hair curlers.

"Get your cigar?" she asked without interest.

"Sure," said Hopkins, "and I knocked around a while

---

21  A *kennel* is a place where animals, especially dogs, are kept.

outside. It's a nice night."

He sat upon the sofa, took out the stump of his cigar, and lit it. Then he gazed at the graceful figures in *The Storm* on the opposite wall.

"I was telling you," he said, "about Mr. Whipple's suit. It's solid gray, and it looks fine."

## INSIGHTS

There are many stories of chivalrous behavior—of brave knights fighting for the honor of virtuous ladies. Chivalry largely disappeared at the end of the Middle Ages, in the 1400s. By about 1600, the Spanish author Miguel de Cervantes was ridiculing chivalry in his novel *Don Quixote.*

But other writers have continued to write about chivalry in a serious, romantic way up to the present day. For example, Sir Walter Scott (1771–1832) glamorized medieval times and ways in novels like *Ivanhoe.*

America was colonized too late to adopt much of the European chivalric tradition. So its writers have tended not to take chivalry seriously. The 19th-century author Mark Twain ridiculed the Middle Ages in many works, including *A Connecticut Yankee in King Arthur's Court.*

And in "The Complete Life of John Hopkins," O. Henry has his own fun with knightly conduct. John Hopkins tries to be a "knight in shining armor" to a wealthy, spoiled New York lady. He loses his fight, but he'll probably always enjoy the memory of having tried.

# A Retrieved Reformation

## VOCABULARY PREVIEW

Below is a list of words that appear in the story. Read the list and get to know the words before you start the story.

**accomplices**—persons associated with another, especially in wrongdoing

**balked**—stopped short and refused to proceed

**clemency**—leniency; mercy

**commotion**—an agitated disturbance; noisy confusion

**convulsions**—abnormal violent and involuntary muscle contractions

**duplicate**—to produce something equal to an original

**frantic**—emotionally out of control; extremely upset

**hesitated**—paused; delayed

**hysterically**—in an extremely emotional manner

**prosperity**—the condition of being successful or thriving; economic well-being

**reformation**—the act of changing for the better; improvement

**rehabilitate**—to bring to a condition of useful and constructive activity

**retrieved**—gotten back again; recovered

**shortcomings**—defects; flaws

**shrieking**—crying out in a high-pitched voice

**unobtrusively**—not readily noticeable; casually

# A Retrieved Reformation

*What could possibly make a safecracker like*
*Dandy Jim Valentine decide to go straight?*
*And could he really change his ways?*

A guard came to the prison shoe shop, where Jimmy Valentine was busily stitching shoes. The guard escorted him to the front office. There the warden handed Jimmy his pardon, which had been signed that morning by the governor.[1]

Jimmy took it in a tired kind of way. He had served nearly ten months of a four-year sentence. He had expected to stay only about three months, at the longest. Jimmy Valentine had many friends on the outside. When a man like that is put in jail, it is hardly worthwhile to even cut his hair.

"Now, Valentine," said the warden, "you'll go out in the morning. Shape up and make a man of yourself. You're not a bad fellow at heart. Stop cracking safes[2] and live straight."

"Me?" said Jimmy, in surprise. "Why, I never cracked a safe in my life."

"Oh, no," laughed the warden. "Of course not. Let's see, now. How was it you happened to get sent up the river[3] on that Springfield job? Was it because you couldn't use your alibi? Were you afraid the truth would hurt somebody in really high society? Or was it simply a case of a mean old jury that had it in for you? It's always one or the other with you innocent victims."

"Me?" said Jimmy, with a blank, innocent look. "Why, warden, I never was in Springfield in my life!"

---

1   A *pardon* is the release from the legal penalties of a crime.
2   Breaking into safes is called "cracking" them.
3   To "get sent up the river" means to go to jail.

"Take him back, Cronin," smiled the warden. "Fix him up with clothes for leaving. Unlock him at 7:00 in the morning, and let him come to the bullpen.[4] Better think over my advice, Valentine."

At 7:15 the next morning, Jimmy stood in the warden's outer office. He had on a suit of poorly fitting, ready-made clothes. He wore a pair of the stiff, squeaky shoes that the state gives its unwilling guests when they are released.

The clerk handed him a railroad ticket and a five-dollar bill. With that, the law expected him to **rehabilitate** himself into good citizenship and **prosperity**.

The warden gave him a cigar and shook hands. Valentine 9762 was listed on the books as "Pardoned by Governor." Then Mr. James Valentine walked out into the sunshine.

Jimmy ignored the song of the birds, the waving green trees, and the smell of the flowers. He headed straight for a restaurant. There he tasted the first sweet joys of liberty—a broiled chicken and a better cigar than the one the warden had given him.

From the restaurant, he proceeded to the train station at an easy pace. He tossed a quarter into the hat of a blind man sitting by the door and boarded his train. Three hours later, he was let off in a little town near the state line. He went to the café of Mike Dolan and shook hands with Mike, who was alone behind the bar.

"Sorry we couldn't make it sooner, Jimmy, me boy," said Mike. "But we had that protest from Springfield to fight, and the governor nearly **balked**. Feeling all right?"

"Fine," said Jimmy. "Got my key?"

Jimmy got his key and went upstairs, unlocking the door of a room at the rear. Everything was just as he had left it. Ben Price's collar button was still there on the floor. It had been torn from that famous detective's shirt when they had overpowered Jimmy to arrest him.

Jimmy pulled a folding bed out from the wall. Then he slid back a panel in the wall and dragged out a dust-covered suitcase. He opened the suitcase and gazed fondly at the finest set of burglar's tools in the East.

---

4   A *bullpen* is a place where prisoners are held temporarily.

It was a complete set of tools, made of specially tempered steel.[5] It included the latest designs in drills, punches, braces and bits,[6] jimmies,[7] clamps, and augers.[8] There were also two or three special tools invented by Jimmy himself, in which he took pride. It had cost him over 900 dollars to have them made.

In half an hour Jimmy went downstairs and through the café. He was now dressed in tasteful and well-fitting clothes. He carried his dusted and cleaned suitcase in his hand.

"Got anything going?" asked Mike Dolan, pleasantly.

"Me?" said Jimmy in a puzzled tone. "I don't understand. I'm representing the New York Amalgamated Short Snap Biscuit Cracker and Frazzled Wheat Company."

This statement delighted Mike. He insisted that Jimmy take a soft drink on the spot. Jimmy never touched alcohol.

A week after the release of Valentine 9762, there was a neat job of safe burglary. It was done in Richmond, Indiana, and there was no clue to the author. The robber only got 800 dollars.

Two weeks after that, there was another burglary, to the tune of 1,500 dollars. A patented,[9] improved, burglarproof safe in Logansport was opened like a bottle. The valuable papers and silver were left untouched.

That began to interest the outlaw catchers. Then an old-fashioned bank safe in Jefferson City became active like a volcano. It threw an eruption of money amounting to 5,000 dollars out of its crater.

The losses were now high enough to bring the matter to Ben Price's attention. By comparing notes, he noticed a remarkable similarity in the methods of the burglaries. So Ben Price investigated the scenes of the robberies.

"That's Dandy Jim Valentine's signature," Price was heard to remark. "He's back in business. Look at that combination

---

5   Tempered steel has been heated and cooled in a way that makes it stronger and harder.

6   A *brace and bit* is a type of hand drill.

7   A *jimmy* is a short bar with curved ends, used to pry things open.

8   An *auger* is a tool for boring holes.

9   The government grants a *patent* to inventors. Something patented is supposedly a newer, better design and cannot be legally copied by others.

knob—jerked out as easy as pulling up a radish in wet weather. He's got the only clamps that can do it. And look how clean those tumblers[10] were punched out! Jimmy never has to drill but one hole. Yes, I guess I want Mr. Valentine. He'll do his full sentence next time, without any short time or **clemency** foolishness."

Ben Price knew Jimmy's habits. He had learned them while working up the Springfield case. Valentine made long jumps between jobs, made quick getaways, and had no **accomplices**. He also had a taste for good society. These ways had helped Mr. Valentine to become known as a successful dodger of punishments.

The word was spread that Ben Price was on the trail of the slippery cracksman. After that, other people with burglarproof safes felt more at ease.

One afternoon, Jimmy Valentine and his suitcase climbed out of the mail coach[11] in Elmore, a little town five miles off the railroad down in the backcountry of Arkansas. Looking like an athletic young senior just home from college, Jimmy went down the board sidewalk toward the hotel.

A young lady crossed the street and passed him at the corner. She entered a door over which hung the sign "The Elmore Bank." Jimmy Valentine looked into her eyes and forgot what he was. He became another man. She lowered her eyes and blushed slightly. Young men of Jimmy's style and looks were scarce in Elmore.

A boy was loafing on the steps of the bank as if he were one of the owners. Jimmy began to ask him questions about the town, feeding him dimes from time to time. Soon the young lady came out. Looking royally unaware of the young man with the suitcase, she went her way.

"Isn't that young lady Miss Polly Simpson?" asked Jimmy. His voice had the false ring of honesty.

"Naw," said the boy. "She's Annabel Adams. Her pa owns this bank. What'd you come to Elmore for? Is that a gold watch

---

10 In a lock, the *tumbler* releases the bolt when moved by a handle or key.

11 The *mail coach* was a stagecoach that picked up and delivered mail.

chain? I'm going to get a bulldog. Got any more dimes?"

Jimmy went to the Planters' Hotel, registered as Ralph D. Spencer, and took a room. He leaned on the desk and told his story to the clerk. He said he had come to Elmore to look for a location to go into business. He had thought of the shoe business. How was the shoe business in the town now? Was there an opening?

The clerk was impressed by Jimmy's clothes and manner. He, himself, was something of a model of fashion to the barely stylish youth of Elmore. But he now saw his own **shortcomings**. He kept trying to figure how Jimmy tied his four-in-hand.[12]

The clerk politely gave Jimmy information. Yes, there ought to be a good opening in the shoe line. There wasn't a real shoe store in the place. The clothes stores and general stores handled them. Business in all lines was fairly good. He said he hoped Mr. Spencer would decide to locate in Elmore. He would find it a pleasant town to live in and the people very friendly.

Mr. Spencer thought he would stay in town a few days and look over the situation. No, the clerk needn't call the boy, he said. He would carry up his suitcase himself. It was rather heavy.

The flame of Jimmy's sudden and unusual attack of love left ashes behind. And Mr. Ralph Spencer was the phoenix that arose from Jimmy Valentine's ashes.[13] He remained in Elmore and prospered. He opened a shoe store and had a good business.

Socially, he was also a success and made many friends. And he got what his heart most desired. He met Miss Annabel Adams and became more and more taken by her charms.

At the end of a year, the situation of Mr. Ralph Spencer was good. He had won the respect of the community. His shoe store was doing very well. And he and Annabel were engaged to be married in two weeks.

Her father, Mr. Adams, was a typical, hardworking country banker who approved of Spencer. Annabel's pride almost equaled her affection. Spencer was as much at home in the

---

12  A *four-in-hand* is a necktie tied in a slipknot with long ends overlapping vertically in front.

13  In Egyptian mythology, a *phoenix* is a bird that is consumed by fire and reborn from its ashes.

family of Mr. Adams as if he were already a member. And he was just as welcome in the home of Annabel's married sister.

One day Jimmy sat down in his room and wrote a letter. He mailed it to the safe address of one of his old friends in St. Louis.

> *Dear Old Pal:*
> *I want you to be at Sullivan's place in Little Rock next Wednesday night at 9:00. I want you to wind up some little matters for me. And also, I want to make you a present of my kit of tools. I know you'll be glad to get them—you couldn't* **duplicate** *them for a thousand dollars. Say, Billy, I've quit the old business—a year ago. I've got a nice store. I'm making an honest living, and I'm going to marry the finest girl on Earth two weeks from now. It's the only life, Billy—the straight one. I wouldn't touch a dollar of another man's money now for a million.*
> *After I get married, I'm going to sell out and go West. There won't be so much danger of having old scores brought up against me. I tell you, Billy, she's an angel. She believes in me, and I wouldn't do another crooked thing for the whole world. Be sure to be at Sully's, for I must see you. I'll bring the tools along with me.*
> *Your old friend,*
> *Jimmy*

On the Monday night after Jimmy wrote this letter, Ben Price arrived **unobtrusively** into Elmore in a hired buggy. He hung around town in his quiet way until he found out what he wanted to know. From the drugstore across the street from Spencer's shoe store he got a good look at Ralph D. Spencer.

"Going to marry the banker's daughter are you, Jimmy?" said Ben to himself, softly. "Well, I don't know!"

The next morning, Jimmy had breakfast at the Adamses'. He was going to Little Rock that day to order his wedding suit.

And he would buy something nice for Annabel. That would be the first time he had left town since he came to Elmore. It had been more than a year now since those last professional jobs. He thought he could safely risk going out.

After breakfast, quite a family party went downtown together. There was Mr. Adams, Annabel, and Jimmy. With them went Annabel's married sister and her two little girls, ages five and nine.

They came to the hotel where Jimmy still boarded, and he ran up to his room. He brought down his suitcase, and then they went on to the bank. There stood Jimmy's horse and buggy, along with Dolph Gibson. He was going to drive Jimmy over to the railroad station.

All went inside, and then behind the high, carved oak railing into the banking room. Jimmy was included, for Mr. Adams's future son-in-law was welcome anywhere. The clerks were pleased to be greeted by the good-looking, agreeable young man who was going to marry Miss Annabel.

Jimmy set his suitcase down. Annabel's heart was bubbling with happiness and lively youth. She put on Jimmy's hat and picked up the suitcase.

"Wouldn't I make a nice drummer?"[14] said Annabel. "My, Ralph! How heavy it is. Feels like it's full of gold bricks."

"Lot of nickel-plated shoe horns in there," said Jimmy, coolly. "I'm going to return them. Thought I'd save express charges by taking them myself. I'm getting awfully careful about money."

The Elmore Bank had just put in a new safe and vault.[15] Mr. Adams was very proud of it and insisted on an inspection by everyone. The vault was a small one, but it had a new patented door. It fastened with three solid steel bolts thrown at the same time with a single handle. It also had a time lock.[16]

Mr. Adams cheerfully explained its workings to Mr. Spencer.

---

14  A *drummer* is a traveling salesperson—one who drums up business.

15  A *vault* is a heavily secured room or area for the safekeeping of valuables.

16  A lock controlled by a clock is called a *time lock*. It cannot be opened before a set time.

Ralph Spencer showed a courteous—but not too great—interest. The two children, May and Agatha, were delighted by the shining metal, funny clock, and knobs.

While they were doing this, Ben Price strolled in. He leaned on his elbow, looking casually inside the railing. He told the teller that he didn't want anything. He was just waiting for a man he knew.

Suddenly there was a scream or two from the women and a **commotion**. May, the nine-year-old girl, had playfully shut Agatha inside the vault. This had been unnoticed by the adults. Then May had shot the bolts and turned the knob of the combination as she had seen Mr. Adams do.

The old banker sprang to the handle and tugged at it for a moment. "The door can't be opened," he groaned. "The clock hasn't been wound or the combination set."

Agatha's mother screamed again, **hysterically**.

"Hush!" said Mr. Adams, raising his trembling hand. "All be quiet for a moment." He called as loudly as he could. "Agatha! Listen to me."

During the following silence they could just hear a faint sound. The child was wildly **shrieking** in the dark vault in a panic of terror.

"My precious darling!" wailed the mother. "She will die of fright! Open the door! Oh, break it open! Can't you men do something?"

"There isn't a man nearer than Little Rock who can open that door," said Mr. Adams in a shaky voice. "My God! Spencer, what shall we do? That child—she can't stand it long in there. There isn't enough air. And besides, she'll go into **convulsions** from fright."

Agatha's mother was **frantic** now. She beat the door of the vault with her hands. Somebody wildly suggested dynamite. Annabel turned to Jimmy, her large eyes full of pain. But she had not yet given up hope. To a woman, nothing seems quite impossible for the man she worships.

"Can't you do something, Ralph? Try, won't you?"

He looked at her with a strange, soft smile on his lips and in his bright eyes.

"Annabel," he said, "give me that rose you are wearing, will you?"

Hardly believing that she heard him right, Annabel unpinned the bud from her dress. She placed it in his hand. Jimmy stuffed it into his vest pocket, threw off his coat and pulled up his shirt-sleeves. With that act, Ralph D. Spencer passed away and Jimmy Valentine took his place.

"Get away from the door, all of you," he commanded sharply. He set his suitcase on the table and opened it out flat. From that time on, he seemed to be unaware of the presence of anyone else.

Jimmy laid out the odd, shining tools swiftly and neatly. He was whistling softly to himself as he always did when at work. In a deep silence and without moving, the others watched him. They seemed to be under a spell.

In a minute Jimmy's pet drill was biting smoothly into the steel door. In ten minutes—breaking his own burglary record—he threw back the bolts and opened the door.

Agatha was almost fainting, but safe. She was gathered into her mother's arms.

Jimmy Valentine put on his coat and walked toward the front door. As he went, he thought he heard a faraway voice that he once knew call, "Ralph!" But he never **hesitated**.

At the door a big man stood somewhat in his way. "Hello, Ben!" said Jimmy, still with his strange smile. "Got around at last, have you? Well, let's go. I don't know that it makes much difference now."

And then Ben Price acted rather strangely.

"Guess you're mistaken, Mr. Spencer," he said. "Don't believe I recognize you. Your buggy's waiting for you, ain't it?"

And Ben Price turned and strolled down the street.

## INSIGHTS

You might say that O. Henry was actually born in prison. The author's real name was William Sidney Porter. As a young man, he held many different jobs. One of those was teller—an employee who receives and pays out money—in an Austin, Texas, bank.

In 1896, two years after he had left that job, Porter was accused of embezzling, or stealing, bank funds. He fled the country, traveling to Honduras and South America. In 1897, he returned, stood trial, and was convicted. (There has been a lot of debate over whether he was really guilty.)

Porter was sent to a federal penitentiary in Ohio. While in jail, he began to write stories under various names—one of which was O. Henry. The stories began to sell. When he was released for good behavior in 1901, Porter changed his name to O. Henry and kept on writing. Many of his stories show an affection for characters who have done time in prison.

In "A Retrieved Reformation," O. Henry says, "Jimmy never touched alcohol." After he became successful, the author, himself, had a problem with heavy drinking. Perhaps he felt that a real hero would not abuse alcohol.

# The Last Leaf

## VOCABULARY PREVIEW

The following words appear in the story. Review the list and get to know the words before you read the story.

**acute**—severe; serious
**chivalric**—honorable; courteous
**contempt**—disgust; disrespect
**contentedly**—happily; satisfyingly
**curative**—healing; restoring
**gnarled**—twisted; knotted
**imported**—brought; transported
**persistent**—determined; continuous
**prowling**—searching; seeking
**quaint**—pleasantly old-fashioned; unique
**scoffed**—ridiculed; sneered
**scorn**—disgust; contempt
**wielded**—handled; employed

# The Last Leaf

*Johnsy was sure that she would die when the*
*last leaf fell.*

In a little district west of Washington Square,[1] the streets have run crazy and broken themselves into small strips called "places." These "places" make strange angles and curves. One street crosses itself a time or two.

An artist once discovered a valuable possibility in this street. Suppose a collector with a bill for paints, paper, and canvas should follow this route. He might suddenly meet himself coming back—without a cent having been paid on the account!

So the art people soon came **prowling** to **quaint**, old Greenwich Village. They were hunting for north windows[2] and 18th-century gables[3] and Dutch attics and low rent. Then they **imported** some pewter mugs and a chafing dish[4] or two from Sixth Avenue and became a colony.[5]

At the top of a squatty, three-story brick building, Sue and Johnsy had their studio. "Johnsy" was a nickname for Joanna. One was from Maine; the other from California. They had met at the table d'hôte[6] of an Eighth Street restaurant called Delmonico's. They found their tastes in art, chicory salad,[7] and fashion so similar that they decided to rent a joint studio.

That was in May. In November, a cold, unseen stranger

---

1 Washington Square Park is in a part of New York City called Greenwich Village. The neighborhood was once a popular place for artists and students because of its low rent.

2 Windows on the north side of a building provide good, strong light that is not too bright and is often preferred by painters.

3 A *gable* is the vertical triangular end of a building from eaves to ridge.

4 A *chafing dish* is a utensil for cooking or keeping food warm.

5 O. Henry is comparing the artists to the colonists of Early America.

6 *Table d'hôte* means "the host's table." It refers to a table open to all guests at a hotel or restaurant, usually for a fixed-price meal.

7 The leaves of chicory plants can be used in salads.

whom the doctors called Pneumonia[8] stalked about the colony, touching one here and there with his icy fingers. Over on the East Side, this terror strode boldly, striking his victims by scores.[9] But his feet tromped slowly through the maze of the narrow and moss-grown "places."

Mr. Pneumonia was not what you call a **chivalric** old gentleman. A little woman with blood thinned by California breezes was hardly fair game for the red-fisted, short-breathed old duffer.[10] But he struck Johnsy. She lay scarcely moving on her bed, looking through the small Dutch windowpanes at the blank side of the next brick house.

One morning the busy doctor indicated to Sue with a shaggy gray eyebrow that he wanted to see her in the hallway.

"She has one chance in—let us say, ten," he said as he shook down the mercury in his thermometer. "And that chance is for her to want to live. The way people are lining up on the side of the undertaker makes the entire pharmacopeia[11] look silly. Your little lady has made up her mind that she's not going to get well. Has she anything on her mind?"

"She—she wanted to paint the Bay of Naples someday," said Sue.

"Paint?—bosh! Has she anything on her mind worth thinking about twice—a man, for instance?"

"A man?" said Sue, with a Jew's harp[12] twang in her voice. "Is a man worth—? But, no, doctor, there is nothing of the kind."

"Well, it is the weakness, then," said the doctor. "I will do all that science can accomplish. But whenever my patient begins to count the carriages in her funeral procession, I subtract 50 percent from the **curative** power of medicines. Perhaps you can get her to ask one question about the new winter styles in coat sleeves. Then I will promise you a one-in-five chance for her, instead of one-in-ten."

---

8   *Pneumonia* is a disease of the lungs. Some forms are mild, others deadly. Now pneumonia can be treated with antibiotics.

9   A *score* is 20 of something.

10  A *duffer* is a stupid or worthless person.

11  Here, *pharmacopeia* refers to the whole collection of medicinal drugs.

12  A *Jew's harp* is a small metal musical instrument that is held between the teeth and plucked to produce a soft, twanging sound.

After the doctor had gone, Sue went into the workroom and cried a paper napkin to a pulp. Then she marched into Johnsy's room with her drawing board, whistling a ragtime[13] tune.

Johnsy lay scarcely making a ripple under the covers, with her face toward the window. Sue stopped whistling, thinking her friend was asleep.

She arranged her board and began a pen-and-ink drawing to illustrate a magazine story. Young artists must pave their way to art by drawing pictures for magazine stories that young authors write to pave their way to literature.

Sue was sketching a pair of elegant horse-show riding trousers and a monocle[14] on the figure of the hero, an Idaho cowboy. She heard a low sound, several times repeated. She went quickly to the bedside.

Johnsy's eyes were open wide. She was looking out the window and counting—counting backward.

"Twelve," she said, and a little later "eleven." And then "ten" and "nine." And then "eight" and "seven" almost together.

Sue looked uneasily out the window. What was there to count? There was only a bare, dreary yard to be seen and the blank side of the brick house 20 feet away. An old ivy vine, **gnarled** and decayed at the roots, climbed halfway up the brick wall. The cold breath of autumn had stricken its leaves from the vine. Its skeleton branches clung, almost bare, to the crumbling bricks.

"What is it, dear?" asked Sue.

"Six," said Johnsy, in almost a whisper. "They're falling faster now. Three days ago there were almost a hundred. It made my head ache to count them. But now it's easy. There goes another one. There are only five left now."

"Five what, dear? Tell your Sudie."

"Leaves. On the ivy vine. When the last one falls, I must go too. I've known that for three days. Didn't the doctor tell you?"

"Oh, I never heard of such nonsense," complained Sue, with magnificent **scorn**. "What have old ivy leaves to do with your

---

13  *Ragtime* is a style of jazz music with "ragged" or off-beat rhythm. It was especially popular in the United States from 1896 to 1917.

14  A *monocle* is an eyeglass for just one eye.

getting well? And you used to love that vine so, you naughty girl. Don't be a goose. Why, the doctor told me this morning that your chances for getting well real soon were—let's see exactly what he said. He said the chances were ten-to-one? Why that's almost as good a chance as we have in New York when we ride on the streetcars or walk past a new building."

"Try to take some broth now," she continued, "and let Sudie go back to her drawing. She can sell it to the editor man and buy port wine for her sick child and pork chops for her greedy self."

"You needn't get any more wine," said Johnsy, keeping her eyes fixed out the window. "There goes another. No, I don't want any broth. That leaves just four. I want to see the last one fall before it gets dark. Then I'll go too."

"Johnsy, dear," said Sue, bending over her, "will you promise me to keep your eyes closed and not look out the window until I am done working? I must hand those drawings in tomorrow. I need the light, or I would draw the shade down."

"Couldn't you draw in the other room?" asked Johnsy coldly.

"I'd rather be here by you," said Sue. "Besides, I don't want you to keep looking at those silly leaves."

"Tell me as soon as you have finished," said Johnsy, closing her eyes and lying white and still as a fallen statue. "Because I want to see the last one fall. I'm tired of waiting. I'm tired of thinking. I want to turn loose my hold on everything and go sailing down, down, just like one of those poor leaves."

"Try to sleep," said Sue. "I must call Behrman up to be my model for the old hermit miner. I'll not be gone a minute. Don't try to move till I come back."

Old Behrman was a painter who lived on the ground floor beneath them. He was past 60 and had a Michelangelo's Moses beard.[15] It curled down from what seemed to be the head of a satyr[16] and along the body of an imp.

Behrman was a failure in art. For 40 years he had **wielded** the brush without getting near enough to touch the hem of

---

15  A Michelangelo's Moses beard refers to the long, flowing beard as seen on the famous sculpture of Moses created by artist Michelangelo Buonarroti (1475–1564).

16  A *satyr* is a mythical woodland creature with pointed ears.

his Mistress's robe.[17] He had been always about to paint a masterpiece, but he had painted nothing except now and then a smudge in the line of business or advertising. He earned a little by serving as a model to those young artists in the colony who could not pay the price of a professional. He drank too much gin and still talked of his coming masterpiece. For the rest, he was a fierce, little old man who **scoffed** terribly at softness in anyone. He regarded himself as a special mastiff-in-waiting[18] to protect the two young artists in the studio above.

Sue found Behrman smelling strongly of juniper berries[19] in his dimly lighted den below. In one corner was a blank canvas on an easel that had been waiting there for 25 years to receive the first line of the masterpiece. She told him of Johnsy's idea. She said she feared Johnsy would indeed, light and fragile as a leaf herself, float away when her slight hold upon the world grew weaker.

Old Behrman, with his red eyes plainly streaming, shouted his **contempt** and scorn for such idiotic imaginings.

"Vass!"[20] he cried. "Is dere people in de world mit der foolishness to die because leafs dey drop off from a cursed vine? I haf not heard of such a thing. No, I will not pose as a model for your fool hermit-dunderhead.[21] Vy do you allow dot silly business to come in de brain of her? Ach, dot poor leetle Miss Yohnsy."[22]

"She is very ill and weak," said Sue, "and the fever has left her mind gloomy and full of strange ideas. Very well, Mr. Behrman, if you do not care to pose for me, you needn't. But I think you are a horrid old—old flibbertigibbet.[23]

---

17 "His Mistress" refers to the artist's muse—or source of inspiration. In Greek mythology, each of the nine muses presided over a different art or science.

18 A *mastiff* is one of a breed of big, strong dogs. Behrman sees himself as a guard dog for the young women.

19 The alcoholic drink gin gets its taste from juniper berries. Junipers are evergreen trees or shrubs.

20 Behrman has a German accent. "Vass" is "what" with a German accent.

21 "Dunderhead" refers to someone who is dumb; a dunce.

22 "Is there people in the world with the foolishness to die because leaves they drop off from a cursed vine? I have not heard of such a thing. No, I will not pose as a model for your fool hermit-dunderhead. Why do you allow that silly business to come in the brain of her? Ach, that poor little Miss Johnsy."

23 A *flibbertigibbet* is a silly, restless person.

"You are just like a woman!" yelled Behrman. "Who said I will not bose? Go on. I come mit you. For half an hour I haf peen trying to say dot I am ready to bose. Is not any place in which one so goot as Miss Yohnsy shall lie sick. Someday I vill baint a masterpiece, and ve shall all go away. Yes."[24]

Johnsy was sleeping when they went upstairs. Sue pulled the shade down to the windowsill and motioned Behrman into the other room. In there they peered out the window fearfully at the ivy vine. Then they looked at each other for a moment without speaking. A **persistent** cold rain was falling, mixed with snow. Behrman, in his old blue shirt, took his seat as the hermit-miner on an upturned kettle for a rock.

When Sue awoke the next morning, she found Johnsy with dull, wide-open eyes staring at the drawn green shade.

"Pull it up; I want to see," she ordered in a whisper.

Wearily, Sue obeyed.

But, look! After the beating rain and fierce gusts of wind that had lasted through the whole night, there yet stood out against the brick wall one ivy leaf. It was the last on the vine. Still dark green near its stem, its jagged edges were tinted with the yellow of death and decay. It hung bravely from a branch some 20 feet above the ground.

"It is the last one," said Johnsy. "I thought it would surely fall during the night. I heard the wind. It will fall today, and I shall die at the same time."

"Dear, dear!" said Sue, leaning her worn face down to the pillow. "Think of me if you won't think of yourself. What would I do?"

But Johnsy did not answer. The lonesomest thing in all the world is a soul when it is making ready to go on its mysterious far journey. The more the idea of dying possessed her, the looser her ties to friendship and the earth became.

The day wore away, and even through the twilight they could see the lone ivy leaf clinging to its stem against the wall. And

---

24 "Who said I will not pose? Go on. I come with you. For half an hour I have been trying to say that I am ready to pose. Is not any place in which one so good as Miss Johnsy shall lie sick. Someday I will paint a masterpiece, and we shall all go away. Yes."

then, with the coming of the night, the north wind was again let loose. The rain still beat against the windows and pattered down from the low Dutch eaves.

When it was light enough, Johnsy the Merciless commanded that the shade be raised.

The ivy leaf was still there.

Johnsy lay for a long time looking at it. And then she called to Sue, who was stirring her chicken broth over the gas stove.

"I've been a bad girl, Sudie," said Johnsy. "Something has made that last leaf stay there to show me how wicked I was. It is a sin to want to die. You may bring me a little broth now and some milk with a little port in it and—no. Bring me a hand mirror first and then pack some pillows around me. I will sit up and watch you cook."

An hour later she said, "Sudie, someday I hope to paint the Bay of Naples."

The doctor came in the afternoon, and Sue made an excuse to go into the hallway as he left.

"Even chances," said the doctor, taking Sue's thin, shaking hand in his. "With good nursing, you'll win. And now I must see another case I have downstairs. Behrman, his name is—some kind of artist, I believe. Pneumonia too. He is an old, weak man, and the attack is **acute**. There is no hope for him. But he goes to the hospital today to be made comfortable."

The next day the doctor said to Sue, "She's out of danger. You've won. Nutrition and care now—that's all."

And that afternoon Sue came to the bed where Johnsy lay. She was **contentedly** knitting a very blue and very useless woolen shoulder scarf. Sue put one arm around her, pillows and all.

"I have something to tell you, white mouse," she said. "Mr. Behrman died of pneumonia today in the hospital. He was ill only two days. The janitor found him on the morning of the first day in his room downstairs, helpless with pain. His shoes and clothing were wet through and icy cold. They couldn't imagine where he had been on such a dreadful night. And then they found a lantern, still lighted, and a ladder that had been dragged from its place. And some scattered brushes, and a palette with green and yellow colors mixed on it, and—

"Look out the window, dear," Sue continued, "at the last ivy leaf on the wall. Didn't you wonder why it never fluttered or moved when the wind blew? Ah, darling, it's Behrman's masterpiece—he painted it there the night that the last leaf fell."

## INSIGHTS

During the 1900s, many artists and writers adopted the motto, "Art for art's sake." By this, they meant that art shouldn't preach or moralize. It should simply be beautiful. Artists and writers who believed and practiced this idea this were known as "aesthetes." Among them were authors like Edgar Allan Poe (1809–1849) and painters like James McNeill Whistler (1834–1903).

It is often said that art imitates life. But to the aesthetes, the truth was just the opposite. They believed that life itself should be made as beautiful as possible—that it should imitate beautiful works of art.

By the time O. Henry wrote "The Last Leaf," the idea of "art for art's sake" was dying out. But the painter Old Behrman clearly still believes in it. His "masterpiece," a painted leaf, is more precious than a real leaf in its way. Because it cannot die, it does what a real leaf could not do. It inspires Johnsy to live.

# The Hypotheses of Failure

## VOCABULARY PREVIEW

Below is a list of words that appear in the story. Read the list and get to know the words before you start the story.

**catastrophe**—tragedy; disaster

**clients**—persons who engage the professional advice or services of another

**complications**—difficult situations

**hypotheses**—theories; assumptions

**hypothetical**—supposed; imagined

**implications**—suggestions or accusations of something usually unfavorable

**incompatibility**—the state of not being able to exist together

**infatuated**—overly affectionate; obsessed

**intricacy**—entanglement; complexity

**philosopher**—a person who seeks wisdom or enlightenment

**presence**—poise, self-confidence

**subtle**—delicate; strategic

**tactics**—strategies; plans

**tedium**—lack of variety; boredom

**unprejudiced**—neutral; impartial

# The Hypotheses of Failure

*Lawyer Gooch was confident that he understood the problem completely—until he suggested his solution.*

Lawyer Gooch gave his undivided attention to the interesting art of his profession. But he did allow his mind to consider one fantasy. He liked to compare his office suite[1] to the lower part of a ship. There were three lawyer's rooms, with a door opening from one to another. These doors could also be closed.

"Ships," Lawyer Gooch would say, "are built for safety. They have separate watertight sections in their bottoms. If one section springs a leak, it fills with water. But the good ship goes on unhurt. If it weren't for the separating bulkheads,[2] one leak would sink the ship.

"Now it often happens that while I am occupied with **clients**, other clients with conflicting interests come in. Archibald—an office boy with a future—helps me keep them apart. I direct the dangerous crowd to be separated into different rooms. Then I sound the depths of each with my legal plumb line.[3]

"If necessary," he would continue, "some clients may be scooped into the hallway. Then they can be allowed to escape by way of the stairs. We can call these the lee scuppers.[4] This way, the good ship of business is kept afloat. But if the people that support the ship were allowed to mingle freely in her hold,[5]

---

1 A *suite* is a series of connected rooms used for an office or for living.
2 *Bulkheads* are the walls that divide a ship into sections or rooms.
3 When crews of ships and boats measure the depths of the waters they are in, it is called *sounding*. This is done with a plumb line.
4 The *lee* side of a ship is the side that is sheltered from the wind. *Scuppers* are openings in the side of a ship to allow water to run off the deck.
5 The *hold* of a ship is the lower inside space where cargo is stored.

we might be swamped. Ha, ha, ha!"

The law is dry. Good jokes are few. Surely Lawyer Gooch should be permitted to make such a slight tax upon the good property of humor. That way, he can relieve the boredom of briefs, the **tedium** of torts, and the prosiness[6] of processes.[7]

Lawyer Gooch's practice mainly dealt with settling the problems of unfortunate marriages. If a marriage failed through **complications**, he stepped in, soothed, and refereed. If it suffered from **implications**, he readjusted, defended, and supported. If it went so far as cheating, he always got light sentences for his clients.

But Lawyer Gooch was not always such a smart and tricky, well-armed fighter. He was not always ready to cut the chains of love with his two-edged sword. He had been known to build up instead of destroy, to put together instead of separate. He could lead mistaken and foolish ones back to each other instead of scattering the flock.

His well-spoken and moving pleas often sent husband and wife, weeping, back into each other's arms. Often, he coached children very successfully. At the perfect moment (and at a given signal), the child would pipe up.

"Papa," the child would say, "won't you tum home again to me and muvver?"

That would win the day and hold a shaky home together.

**Unprejudiced** people admitted that Lawyer Gooch received big fees from these reunited clients. He made as much as he would have been paid if the cases had been contested in court. Prejudiced people suggested that his fees were actually doubled. That was because the regretful couples always came back later for the divorce, anyhow.

Every June the legal ship of Lawyer Gooch (to borrow his own words) was nearly becalmed.[8] The divorce mill grinds slowly in June. It is the month of Cupid and love.

So Lawyer Gooch sat idle in the middle room of his clientless

---

6  *Prosiness* means wordiness.

7  These are legal terms. A *brief* is a formal listing of all the arguments, facts, evidence, and points of law for a particular case. A *tort* is a damage or injury for which a person can sue another. A *process* is a summons for a witness.

8  A sailing ship is *becalmed* when it is motionless because of lack of wind.

suite. A waiting room connected—or rather separated—this room from the hallway. Archibald was assigned to the waiting room. He received cards, or at least spoken names, from visitors. Then he took this information to his master while the visitors waited.

Suddenly, on this day, there came a great knocking at the outside door.

Archibald opened it and was brushed aside unimportantly by the visitor. Without giving Archibald his due respect, the man went at once into the office of Lawyer Gooch. The visitor threw himself with good-natured forwardness into a comfortable chair that was facing that gentleman.

"You are Phineas C. Gooch, attorney-at-law?" asked the visitor. His tone of voice made his words at once a question, a statement, and an accusation.

Before making any reply, the lawyer sized up his possible client with one of his brief but sharp glances.

The man was of the bold type—large-sized, active, and carefree in appearance. He was vain, beyond a doubt. He looked slightly proud, clever, and at ease. He was well dressed, although a shade too fancy.

The man was seeking a lawyer. But if that fact would seem likely to saddle him with troubles, they were not obvious. His eyes glowed, and he appeared courageous.

"My name is Gooch," the lawyer finally admitted. Under pressure, he would also have confessed to the Phineas C. But he did not consider it good practice to volunteer information. "I did not receive your card," he continued in a reprimanding tone, "so I—"

"I know you didn't," remarked the visitor, coolly. "And you won't just yet. Light up?" He threw a leg over an arm of his chair and tossed a handful of rich-looking cigars upon the table. Lawyer Gooch knew the brand. He thawed just enough to accept the invitation to smoke.

"You are a divorce lawyer," said the cardless visitor.

This time there was no question in his voice. Nor did his words form a simple statement. They formed a complaint—a sign of disapproval. It was like one would say to a dog, "You are a dog."

Lawyer Gooch was silent under the disapproval.

"You handle," continued the visitor, "all the various problems of busted-up marriages. You are a surgeon, we might say. You remove Cupid's darts when he shoots 'em into the wrong parties. The torch of love sometimes burns so low you can't light a cigar at it. But you furnish new bright lights for those dark homes."

"I have taken cases," said the lawyer, carefully, "of the kind to which your figures of speech seem to refer. Do you wish to consult with me professionally, Mr.—" The lawyer paused, obviously waiting.

"Not yet," said the other, with a proud wave of his cigar. "Not just yet. Let us approach the subject carefully. I should have used such caution in the original act that makes this get-together necessary.

"There is a jumbled marriage that needs to be straightened out," he continued. "But before I give you names, I want your honest opinion on the points of the mix-up. Well, anyhow, I want your professional opinion. I want you to size up the **catastrophe**—in general—you understand? I'm Mr. Nobody, and I've got a story to tell you. Then you say what's what. Do you get my message?"

"You want to state a **hypothetical** case?" suggested Lawyer Gooch.

"That's the word I was after. *Apothecary*[9] was the best shot I could make at it in my mind. *Hypothetical* works. I'll state the case. Suppose there's a woman—a really fine-looking woman—who has run away from her husband and home. She has a bad crush on another man. He went to her town to work up some real estate business.

"Now, we may as well call this woman's husband Thomas R. Billings," the man added. "For that's his name. I'm giving you straight tips on the names. The Lothario[10] chap is Henry K. Jessup.

"The Billingses lived in a little town called Susanville—a good many miles from here. Now, Jessup leaves Susanville two

---

9   An *apothecary* is a pharmacist.

10  Lothario was a character in an 18th-century play. His main interest was seducing women.

weeks ago. The next day Mrs. Billings follows him. She's dead gone on this man Jessup. You can bet your law library on that."

Lawyer Gooch's client said this with oily satisfaction. Even the hardened lawyer experienced a slight ripple of disgust. He now saw clearly the vanity of the lady-killer in his visitor. The man had the self-centered smugness of the successful flirt.

"Now," continued the visitor, "suppose this Mrs. Billings wasn't happy at home? We'll say she and her husband didn't go together worth a cent. They've got **incompatibility** to burn. The things she likes, Billings wouldn't have as a gift with trading stamps.[11]

"They fight like cats and dogs all the time," said the client. "She's an educated woman in science and culture. She reads things out loud at meetings. Billings is not up-to-date. He don't appreciate progress and art and ethics—things of that sort. Old Billings is simply a fool when it comes to such things. The lady is out and out above his class.

"Now, lawyer, don't it look like we need a fair balance of rights and wrongs?" asked the man. "Shouldn't a woman like that be allowed to throw down Billings? Shouldn't she take the man that can appreciate her?"

"Incompatibility," said Lawyer Gooch, "is undoubtedly the source of much conflict and unhappiness in marriage. Where it is positively proved, divorce would seem to be the fair remedy. Are you—excuse me—is this man Jessup one to whom the lady may safely trust her future?"

"Oh, you can bet on Jessup," said the client with a confident wag of his head. "Jessup's all right. He'll do the square thing. Why, he left Susanville just to keep people from talking about Mrs. Billings. But she followed him, and now of course he'll stick to her. When she gets a divorce, all legal and proper, Jessup will do the proper thing."

"And now," said Lawyer Gooch, "we'll go on with the hypothesis, if you prefer. Supposing that my services should be desired in the case, what—"

The client rose suddenly to his feet.

---

11 *Trading stamps* were once given with some purchases. The stamps could be collected and traded for certain items.

"Oh, dang the hypothetical business!" he exclaimed impatiently. "Let's let it drop and get down to straight talk. You ought to know who I am by this time. I want that woman to have her divorce. I'll pay for it. The day you set Mrs. Billings free, I'll pay you 500 dollars."

Lawyer Gooch's client banged his fist upon the table to punctuate his generosity.

"If that is the case—" began the lawyer.

"Lady to see you, sir," bawled Archibald just then, bouncing in from his waiting room. He had orders to always announce immediately any client that might come. There was no sense in turning away business.

Lawyer Gooch took client number one by the arm and led him smoothly into one of the connecting rooms.

"Please do me a favor by remaining here a few minutes, sir," he said. "I will return and continue our meeting with the least possible delay. I am expecting a visit from a very wealthy old lady. It is in connection with a will. I will not keep you waiting long."

The breezy gentleman cooperated helpfully, seating himself and taking up a magazine. The lawyer returned to the middle office, carefully closing the connecting door behind him.

"Show the lady in, Archibald," he said to the office boy, who was awaiting the order.

A tall lady with commanding **presence** entered the room. She was both stern and handsome. She wore robes—not clothes, but roomy and flowing robes. In her eyes, the glowing flame of genius and soul could be seen. In her hand was a green bag that was big enough to hold a bushel. Her umbrella also seemed to wear a flowing robe. She accepted a chair.

"Are you Mr. Phineas C. Gooch, the lawyer?" she asked. Her tone was formal and unfriendly.

"I am," answered Lawyer Gooch without any extra words. He was never wordy when dealing with women. He felt that women were wordy and time was wasted when both sides in a discussion used the same **tactics**.

"As a lawyer, sir," began the lady, "you may have gained some knowledge of the human heart. Do you believe that the cowardly and narrow-minded rules of our artificial social life should get in the way? Should they block a noble and affectionate heart? Especially when that heart finds its true mate? When it finds in this world the one among all the miserable and worthless creeps that are called men?"

"Madam," said Lawyer Gooch in the tone that he used for controlling his female clients. "This is an office for conducting the practices of law. I am a lawyer, not a **philosopher**. Nor am I the editor of an 'Answers to the Lovelorn' newspaper column. I have other clients waiting. I will ask you kindly to come to the point."

"Well, you needn't get so stiff around the gills about it," said the lady. Her glowing eyes snapped, and her umbrella made a startling circle. "Business is what I've come for. I want your opinion in the matter of a suit for divorce, as common people would call it. But this is really only a correction of improper and common rules. The shortsighted laws of man have put these difficulties between a loving—"

"I beg your pardon, madam," interrupted Lawyer Gooch with some impatience. "Excuse me for reminding you again that this is a law office. Perhaps Mrs. Wilcox—"

"Mrs. Wilcox is all right," cut in the lady with a hint of bitterness. "And so are Tolstoy and Mrs. Gertrude Atherton and Omar Khayyam and Mr. Edward Bok.[12] I've read 'em all. I would like to discuss with you the divine right of the soul. I would like to talk about its opposite—the freedom-destroying rules of a prejudiced and narrow-minded society.

"But I will proceed to business," the woman added. "I would prefer to lay the matter before you in an impersonal way until you judge its value. That is, to describe it as a fictional example, without—"

"You wish to state a hypothetical case?" said Lawyer Gooch.

"I was going to say that," said the lady sharply. "Now, suppose there is a woman who is all soul and heart. She desires

---

12  Ella Wheeler Wilcox (1850–1919) was an American poet. Perhaps her most famous lines are "Laugh, and the world laughs with you; / Weep, and you weep alone." Count Leo Tolstoy (1828–1910) was a Russian novelist. Gertrude Atherton (1857–1948) was an American novelist. Omar Khayyam (about 1050–1122) was a Persian poet. Edward Bok (1863–1930) was editor of the *Ladies' Home Journal.*

a complete existence. This woman has a husband who is far below her in ability, in taste—in everything. Bah! He is a brute. He despises literature. He sneers at the grand thoughts of the world's great thinkers. He thinks only of real estate and such foul things. He is no mate for a woman with soul.

"We will say," she continued, "that this unfortunate wife one day meets her ideal—a man with brain and heart and energy. She loves him. Although this man feels the thrill of a newfound attraction, he is too noble, too honorable to declare himself. He flies from the presence of his beloved. She flies after him. With a wonderful lack of concern, she tramps upon the chains with which a backward social system would bind her.

"Now, what will a divorce cost?" the woman asked. "Eliza Ann Timmins, the poetess of Sycamore Gap, got one for 340 dollars. Can I—I mean can this lady I speak of—get one that cheap?"

"Madam," said Lawyer Gooch, "your last two or three sentences delight me with their intelligence and clearness. Can we not now abandon the hypothetical? Can we get down to names and business?"

"I should say so!" exclaimed the lady, becoming practical with admirable speed. "Thomas R. Billings is the name of the low brute. He stands between the happiness of his legal—his legal, but not his spiritual—wife and Henry K. Jessup. Jessup is the noble man whom nature intended for Mrs. Billings.

"I," the client finished, as though making a dramatic announcement, "am Mrs. Billings!"

"Gentleman to see you, sir," shouted Archibald, invading the room almost at a handspring. Lawyer Gooch arose from his chair.

"Mrs. Billings," the lawyer said courteously, "allow me to show you into the next office for a few minutes. I am expecting a very wealthy old gentleman on business connected with a will. In a very short while I will join you and continue our discussion."

With his usual polite manner, Lawyer Gooch showed his soulful client out. He took her into the remaining unoccupied room. He came out, closing the door with care.

The next visitor introduced by Archibald was a thin,

nervous, sour-looking man of middle age. He had a worried and fearful expression on his face. He carried in one hand a small alligator-hide bag.

The lawyer placed a chair for the visitor, and the man set down his bag on the floor. His clothing was of good quality, but it appeared to be covered with the dust of travel. He had given no thought to neatness or style.

"You make a specialty of divorce cases," the visitor said. His tone was nervous but businesslike.

"I may say," began Lawyer Gooch, "that my practice has not altogether avoided—"

"I know you do," interrupted client number three. "You needn't tell me. I've heard all about you. I have a case to lay before you, without necessarily disclosing any connection that I might have with it. That is—"

"You wish," said Lawyer Gooch, "to state a hypothetical case."

"You may call it that. I am a plain man of business. I will be as brief as possible. We will first take up the hypothetical woman. We will say she is married unhappily. In many ways she is a superior woman. She is considered to be physically handsome. She is devoted to what she calls literature—poetry and prose and such stuff.

"Her husband is a plain man in the business walks of life. Their home has not been happy, although the husband has tried to make it so. Some time ago, a man—a stranger—came to the peaceful town where they lived. The husband and the stranger were engaged in some real estate operations.

"This woman met this man," the visitor continued. "It is impossible to explain why, but she became **infatuated** with him. Her attentions became obvious. Soon the man felt the community was not a safe place for him, so he left it. She followed him. She left her home, where she was provided with every comfort. She followed this man who had aroused such a strange affection.

"Is there anything sadder," concluded the client in a trembling voice, "than the wrecking of a home by a woman's thoughtless foolishness?"

Lawyer Gooch delivered the cautious opinion that there was not.

"This man she has gone to join," continued the visitor, "is not the man to make her happy. It is a wild and foolish self-deception that makes her think he will. Her husband, in spite of their many disagreements, is the only one capable of dealing with her sensitive and unusual nature. But she does not realize this now."

"Would you consider a divorce the logical cure in the case you present?" asked Lawyer Gooch. He felt that the conversation was wandering too far from his field of business.

"A divorce!" exclaimed the client, feelingly—almost tearfully. "No, no—not that. I have read, Mr. Gooch, of many times when you acted as a go-between for a split-up husband and wife. Your sympathy and kindly interest brought them together again.

"Let us drop the hypothetical case," the visitor suggested. "I no longer need to conceal that it is I who am the sufferer in this very affair. The names you shall have—Thomas R. Billings and wife—and Henry K. Jessup, the man with whom she is infatuated."

Client number three laid his hand upon Mr. Gooch's arm. Deep emotion showed on his troubled face.

"For heaven's sake!" he cried. "Help me in this hour of trouble. Seek out Mrs. Billings. Persuade her to abandon this upsetting pursuit of nonsense. Tell her, Mr. Gooch, that her husband is willing to receive her back to his heart and home. Promise her anything that will persuade her to return.

"I have heard of your success in these matters," the man said. "Mrs. Billings cannot be very far away. I am worn out with travel and weariness. Twice during the pursuit I saw her, but various things prevented our having a talk. Will you undertake this mission for me, Mr. Gooch, and earn my eternal gratitude?"

Lawyer Gooch frowned slightly at the other's last words. But he immediately called up an expression of decent kindness.

"It is true," he said, "that on a number of occasions I have been successful with couples who wanted to cut their marriage bonds. I persuaded them to think better of their rash intentions, and they returned to their homes together.

"But I assure you," Lawyer Gooch added, "that the work is

often very difficult. The amount of argument and determination that it requires would astonish you. And, if I may be allowed to say, it also requires outstanding powers of persuasion. But this is a case into which I would wholly put my heart. I feel deeply for you, sir. I would be most happy to see husband and wife reunited.

"But my time," concluded the lawyer, looking at his watch as if suddenly reminded of the fact, "is valuable."

"I am aware of that," said the client. "If you will take the case, persuade Mrs. Billings to return home, convince her to leave the man alone that she is following. On that day I will pay you the sum of 1,000 dollars. I have made a little money in real estate during the recent boom in Susanville. I will not mind paying that much."

Lawyer Gooch rose and again checked his watch. "Keep your seat for a few moments, please," he said. "I had very nearly forgotten that I have another client waiting in another room. I will return in the briefest possible time."

The situation was now one that fully satisfied Lawyer Gooch's love of **intricacy** and complication. He enjoyed cases that presented such **subtle** problems and possibilities. It pleased him to think that he was master of the fate and happiness of these three individuals. They sat, not knowing of one another's presence, within his reach.

His old idea of the ship glided into his mind. But now the image didn't work. To have filled every section of an actual ship would have been to endanger her safety. But now, his rooms were full. And his ship of business could only sail on to the excellent port of a fine, fat fee. The thing for him to do, of course, was to wring the best bargain he could from one of his anxious passengers.

First Gooch called to the office boy. "Lock the outer door, Archibald, and admit no one."

Then the lawyer moved with long, silent strides into the room in which client number one waited. That gentleman sat patiently scanning the pictures in the magazine. He had a cigar in his mouth and his feet upon a table.

"Well," he remarked cheerfully as the lawyer entered, "have

you made up your mind? Does 500 dollars go for getting the fair lady a divorce?"

"You mean that as a retainer?"[13] asked Lawyer Gooch, softly.

"Huh?" asked the man. "No, for the whole job. It's enough, ain't it?"

"My fee," said Lawyer Gooch, "would be 1,500 dollars. That's 500 dollars down, and the remainder upon the granting of the divorce."

A loud whistle came from client number one. His feet descended to the floor.

"Guess we can't close the deal," he said, arising. "I cleaned up 500 dollars in a little real estate bargain down in Susanville. I'd do anything I could to free the lady, but that is greater than my pile."

"Could you stand 1,200 dollars?" asked the lawyer suggestively.

"I tell you," replied the man, "500 is my limit. Guess I'll have to hunt up a cheaper lawyer." The client put on his hat.

"Out this way, please," said Lawyer Gooch, opening the door that led into the hallway.

The gentleman flowed out of the room and down the stairs.

Lawyer Gooch smiled to himself. "Exit Mr. Jessup," he murmured. He fingered the Henry Clay tuft of hair at his ear.[14] "And now for the abandoned husband." He returned to the middle office and put on a businesslike manner.

"I understand," he said to client number three, "that you agree to pay 1,000 dollars if I am successful. I must bring about, or cause, the return of Mrs. Billings to her home. I must bring about her giving up her infatuated pursuit of the man for whom she has taken such a violent fancy. The case is now absolutely in my hands on that basis. Is that correct?"

"Entirely," said the other eagerly. "And I can produce the cash at two hours' notice."

Lawyer Gooch stood up at his full height. His thin figure

---

13  A *retainer* is a fee paid to reserve the services of a lawyer or other professional.

14  Henry Clay (1777–1852) was a U.S. lawyer and politician during the first half of the 19th century. He had tufts of white hair in front of each ear.

seemed to expand. His thumbs sought the armholes of his vest. Upon his face was a look of sympathetic kindness that he always wore during such times.

"Then, sir," he said in kindly tones, "I think I can promise you an early relief from your troubles. I have that much confidence in my powers of argument and persuasion. I believe in the natural leaning of the human heart toward good and in the strong influence of a husband's unfaltering love. Mrs. Billings, sir, is here—in that room." The lawyer's long arm pointed to the door. "I will call her in at once, and our united pleading—"

Lawyer Gooch paused. Client number three had leaped from his chair as if pushed by steel springs. He clutched at his alligator-hide bag.

"What the devil," he exclaimed harshly, "do you mean? That woman is in there! I thought I shook her off 40 miles back."

He ran to the open window, looked out below, and threw one leg over the sill.

"Stop!" cried Lawyer Gooch in amazement. "What are you doing? Come, Mr. Billings, and face your erring but innocent wife. Our combined appeals cannot fail to—"

"Billings!" shouted the now thoroughly upset client. "I'll Billings you, you old idiot!"

Turning, he hurled his bag with fury at the lawyer's head. It struck that astounded peacemaker between the eyes, causing him to stagger backward a pace or two. When Lawyer Gooch recovered his wits, he saw that his client had disappeared. Rushing to the window, he leaned out and saw the coward.

The man was picking himself up from the top of a shed. He had dropped there from the second-story window. Without stopping to collect his hat, the man jumped down the remaining ten feet to the alley. He flew up the alley with amazing speed, until the surrounding buildings swallowed him up from view.

Lawyer Gooch passed his trembling hand across his brow. It was a habit with him, and it helped clear his thoughts. Perhaps now it also seemed to soothe the spot where a very hard alligator-hide bag had struck.

The bag lay upon the floor, wide open, with its contents spilled about. Without thinking, Lawyer Gooch stooped to gather up the articles. The first was a collar.[15] The all-seeing eye of the man of law perceived, wonderingly, the initials H. K. J. marked upon it. Then came a comb, a brush, a folded map, and a piece of soap. Lastly, a handful of old business letters addressed—every one of them—to "Henry K. Jessup, Esq."

Lawyer Gooch closed the bag and set it upon the table. He hesitated for a moment. Then he put on his hat and walked into the office boy's waiting room.

"Archibald," he said mildly as he opened the hall door, "I am going to the Supreme Court rooms. In five minutes you may step into the inner office. Inform the lady who is waiting there that"—here Lawyer Gooch used common slang—"that there's nothing doing."

---

15  Here, the collar is a detachable collar that can be worn with different dress shirts.

## INSIGHTS

O. Henry liked the idea of coincidences—accidental events or connections that are so unlikely that they almost seem planned. In "The Hypotheses of Failure" three people in a marriage triangle arrive at the same lawyer's office at almost the same time. Other stories in this collection also rely on coincidences, including "The Gift of the Magi." In "A Retrieved Reformation," an unexpected situation forces a reformed bank robber to use his skills and reveal his past.

O. Henry loved the irony—the contrast between appearance and reality—he saw in such coincidences. When the outcome of a situation is the opposite of someone's expectations, that's called *situational irony*. In "The Hypotheses of Failure," several characters face surprise outcomes—Mrs. Billings, Henry Jessup, and Lawyer Gooch, for example.

When the reader has important information that the characters in the story don't know about, that's called *dramatic irony*. For example, did you realize who either of the male clients was before Lawyer Gooch did? Did you guess that Mrs. Billings or Lawyer Gooch was in for a surprise?

# Mammon and the Archer

## VOCABULARY PREVIEW

Below is a list of words that appear in the story. Read the list and get to know the words before you start the story.

**aristocrat**—nobleman; gentleman
**clamor**—a loud, continuous noise
**comradeship**—friendship; companionship
**congested**—overcrowded; jammed
**converging**—meeting; intersecting
**emblem**—symbol; token
**mercenary**—purchased; hired
**mystified**—confused; puzzled
**oppressed**—burdened; weighted down
**quaint**—unique and beautiful
**reverently**—respectfully; solemnly
**ruddy**—reddish; rosy-cheeked
**sentiment**—fond feeling of the past
**straggling**—wandering; traveling

# Mammon and the Archer[1]

*Old Anthony Rockwall was sure he could buy*
*anything for his son, even though everyone*
*insisted that he couldn't buy love.*

Old Anthony Rockwall looked out the library window of his big Fifth Avenue mansion and grinned. He was a retired manufacturer and owner of Rockwall's Eureka Soap. His neighbor to the right was **aristocrat** G. Van Schuylight Suffolk-Jones, a member of many exclusive clubs.

Rockwall watched as his wealthy neighbor came out to his waiting motorcar. As usual, Suffolk-Jones rudely wrinkled his nose at the front of Rockwall's house. The soap palace looked like an Italian Renaissance building.[2]

"Stuck-up old statuette of nothing!" commented the ex-Soap King. "I'll have this house painted red, white, and blue next summer. We'll see if that makes his Dutch nose turn up any higher."

And then Anthony Rockwall went to the door of his library and shouted "Mike!" That same voice had once chipped off pieces of the sky over the Kansas prairies. Rockwall had never cared for bells to summon servants.

"Tell my son," said Anthony to the answering servant, "to come in here before he leaves the house."

When young Rockwall entered the library, the old man laid aside his newspaper. He looked at his son with a kindly but grim expression on his big, smooth, **ruddy** face. He rumpled his mop

---

1  *Mammon* is a term for material wealth or possessions, especially those having a bad influence. The Archer is referring to Cupid, the Roman god of erotic love.

2  During the Italian Renaissance (the 15th and 16th centuries), builders and artists copied the styles of ancient Greece and Rome. For example, an Italian Renaissance building might have columns and other marble decorations on the front.

of white hair with one hand and rattled the keys in his pocket with the other.

"Richard," said Anthony Rockwall, "what do you pay for the soap that you use?"

Richard, only six months home from college, was startled a little. He had not yet taken the measure of[3] this father of his. The old man was full of surprises.

"Six dollars a dozen, I think, Dad."

"And your clothes?"

"I suppose about 60 dollars, as a rule."

"You're a gentleman," said Anthony positively. "I've heard of these young bucks spending 24 dollars a dozen for soap. And they go over the hundred mark for clothes. You've got as much money to waste as any of 'em, and yet you stick to what's decent and moderate.

"Now I use the old Eureka brand," Anthony continued. "Not only for **sentiment**, but it's the purest soap made. Whenever you pay more than 10 cents a cake for soap, you buy bad perfumes and labels. But 50 cents is doing very well for a young man in your generation, position, and condition.

"As I said, you're a gentleman. They say it takes three generations to make one. They're off. Money'll do it as slick as soap. It's made you one. By golly, it's almost made one of me. I'm nearly as impolite and disagreeable and ill-mannered as these two old Dutch gents on each side of me. They can't sleep nights because I bought in between 'em."

"There are some things that money can't do," remarked young Rockwall, rather gloomily.

"Now, don't say that," said old Anthony, shocked. "I bet my money on money every time. I've been through the encyclopedia down to *Y* looking for something you can't buy with it. I expect to have to take up the appendix[4] next week. I'm for money against all the rest. Tell me something money won't buy."

"One thing," answered Richard, looking a little annoyed. "It won't buy one into the exclusive circles of society."

"Oho! Won't it?" thundered the champion of the root of

---

3   To "take the measure of someone" is to figure out something about that person's character—to see how he or she "measures up."

4   The *appendix* of a book is extra material added at the end.

evil. "Where would your exclusive circles be if the first Astor hadn't had the money to pay for his steerage passage[5] over? You tell me."

Richard sighed.

"And that's what I was coming to," said the old man, less roughly. "That's why I asked you to come in. There's something going wrong with you, boy. I've been noticing it for two weeks.

"Out with it," he continued. "I guess I could lay my hands on 11 million within 24 hours, besides the real estate. If it's your liver, there's the *Rambler* down in the bay. The ship is loaded with coal and ready. It can steam down to the Bahamas in two days."

"Not a bad guess, Dad," replied Richard. "You haven't missed it by far."

"Ah," said Anthony, cleverly. "What's her name?"

Richard began to walk up and down the library floor. There was plenty of **comradeship** and sympathy in this crude old father of his. It gave Richard confidence.

"Why don't you ask her?" demanded old Anthony. "She'll jump at you. You've got the money and the looks, and you're a decent boy. Your hands are clean. You've got no Eureka soap on 'em. You've been to college, but she'll overlook that."

"I haven't had a chance," said Richard.

"Make one," said Anthony. "Take her for a walk in the park or on a hayride. Or walk home with her from church. Chance? Nonsense!"

"You don't know the social mill, Dad. She's part of the stream that turns it. Every hour and minute of her time is arranged for days in advance. I must have that girl, Dad, or this town is just a backcountry swamp to me forevermore. And I can't write my feelings—I can't do that."

"Tut!" said the old man. "Do you mean to tell me that with all the money I've got, you can't get an hour or two of a girl's time for yourself?"

---

5    The founder of the Astor family fortune, John Jacob Astor (1763–1848), was born a butcher's son in Germany. He immigrated to the United States at the age of 20. By the time he died, he was the wealthiest man in the country. On a passenger ship, the *steerage* is the less desirable area, where passage is cheapest.

"I've put it off too late," said Richard. "She's going to sail for Europe at noon day after tomorrow for a two years' stay. I'm to see her alone tomorrow evening for a few minutes. She's at her aunt's house now. I can't go there. But I'm allowed to meet her with a cab at the Grand Central Station tomorrow evening, at the 8:30 train.

"We'll drive down Broadway to Wallack's Theater at a gallop," he continued. "Her mother and a party of people who have box seats will be waiting for us in the lobby. Do you think she would listen to a declaration from me during those six or eight minutes, under those circumstances?

"No!" insisted Richard. "And what chance would I have in the theater or afterward? None. No, Dad, this is one tangle that your money can't unravel. We can't buy one minute of time with cash; if we could, rich people would live longer. There's no hope of getting a talk with Miss Lantry before she sails."

"All right, Richard, my boy," said old Anthony cheerfully. "You may run along down to your club now. I'm glad it ain't your liver. But don't forget to honor the great god Money from time to time. You say money won't buy time? Well, of course you can't order eternity wrapped up and delivered at your residence for a price. But I've seen Father Time get pretty bad bruises on his heels when he walked through the gold diggings."

That night, Aunt Ellen visited. She was gentle, sentimental, wrinkled, sighing, and **oppressed** by wealth. She came to see Brother Anthony while he was reading his evening paper. She began to talk on the subject of lovers' woes.

"He told me all about it," said Brother Anthony, yawning. "I told him my bank account was at his service. And then he began to knock money. Said money couldn't help. Said the rules of society couldn't be moved a yard, not even by a team of ten-millionaires."

"Oh, Anthony," sighed Aunt Ellen, "I wish you would not think so much of money. Wealth is nothing where true affection is concerned. Love is all-powerful. If he only had spoken earlier! She could not have refused our Richard. But now I fear it is too late. He will have no opportunity to address her. All your gold cannot bring happiness to your son."

At eight o'clock the next evening, Aunt Ellen took a **quaint**, old gold ring from a badly worn case and gave it to Richard. "Wear it tonight, nephew," she begged. "Your mother gave it to me. She said it brought good luck in love. She asked me to give it to you when you had found the one you loved."

Young Rockwall took the ring **reverently** and tried it on his smallest finger. It slipped as far as the second joint and stopped. He took it off and stuffed it into his vest pocket, after the manner of man. And then he phoned for his cab.

At the station he captured Miss Lantry out of the noisy mob at 8:32.

"We mustn't keep Mamma and the others waiting," she said.

"To Wallack's Theater as fast as you can drive!" said Richard loyally.

They whirled up 42nd to Broadway. Broadway leads from the soft meadows of sunset to the rocky hills of morning. At 34th Street, young Richard quickly thrust up the trapdoor and ordered the cabman to stop.

"I've dropped a ring," he apologized as he climbed out. "It was my mother's, and I'd hate to lose it. I won't delay you a minute. I saw where it fell."

In less than a minute he was back in the cab with the ring. But within that minute, a crosstown car had stopped directly in front of the cab. The cabman tried to pass to the left, but a heavy delivery wagon cut him off. He tried the right and had to back away from a furniture van that had no business being there.

He tried to back out but dropped his reins and complained dutifully. He was blockaded in a tangled mess of vehicles and horses. One of those street blockades had occurred that sometimes tie up business and movement quite suddenly in the big city.

"Why don't you drive on?" said Miss Lantry impatiently. "We'll be late."

Richard stood up in the cab and looked around. He saw a **congested** flood of wagons, trucks, cabs, vans, and streetcars. They filled the vast space where Broadway, 6th Avenue, and 34th Street cross one another. It was just like a 26-inch maiden fills her 22-inch girdle.[6]

---

6   A *girdle* is a woman's close-fitting undergarment that extends from the waist to below the hips.

And still from all the cross streets vehicles were hurrying and rattling toward the **converging** point at full speed. They were hurling themselves into the **straggling** mass, locking wheels and adding their drivers' complaints to the **clamor**.

The entire traffic of Manhattan seemed to have jammed itself around the couple. Thousands of watchers lined the sidewalks. But the oldest New Yorker among them had never seen a street blockade the size of this one.

"I'm very sorry," said Richard, as he sat down again, "but it looks as if we are stuck. They won't get this jumble loosened up in an hour. It was my fault. If I hadn't dropped the ring, we—"

"Let me see the ring," said Miss Lantry. "Now that it can't be helped, I don't care. I think theaters are stupid, anyway."

At 11:00 that night somebody tapped lightly on Anthony Rockwall's door.

"Come in!" shouted Anthony. He was in a red dressing gown, reading a book of pirate adventures.

*Somebody* was Aunt Ellen, looking like a gray-haired angel that had been left on earth by mistake.

"They're engaged, Anthony," she said softly. "She has promised to marry our Richard. On their way to the theater there was a traffic jam. It was two hours before their cab could get out of it.

"And, oh, Brother Anthony," she added, "don't ever boast of the power of money again. A little **emblem** of true love was the cause of our Richard finding his happiness. It was a little ring that stood for unending and not **mercenary** affection. He dropped it in the street and got out to recover it. And before they could continue, the blockade occurred. He spoke to his love and won her there while the cab was hemmed in. Money is garbage compared with true love, Anthony."

"All right," said old Anthony. "I'm glad the boy has got what he wanted. I told him I wouldn't spare any expense in the matter."

"But, Brother Anthony, what good could your money have done?"

"Sister," said Anthony Rockwall, looking down at his book. "I've got my pirate in a devil of a scrape. His ship has just been scuttled.[7] He's too good a judge of the value of money to let it drown. I wish you would let me go on with this chapter."

The story should end here. I wish it would as much as you who read it wish it did. But we must go to the bottom of the well for truth.

The next day a person with red hands and a blue polka-dot necktie arrived at Anthony Rockwall's house. The man, who called himself Kelly, was at once received in the library.

"Well," said Anthony, reaching for his checkbook, "it was a good batch of soap. Let's see—you had 5,000 dollars in cash."

"I paid out 300 dollars more of my own," said Kelly. "I had to go a little above the estimate. I got the express wagons and cabs mostly for three dollars, but the trucks and two-horse teams mostly raised me to ten dollars. The motormen wanted ten, and some of the loaded teams, 20. The cops hit me hardest. I paid two 50 dollars, and the rest 20 and 25.

"But didn't it work beautifully, Mr. Rockwall?" Kelly added. "I'm glad William A. Brady[8] wasn't onto that little outdoor vehicle mob scene. I wouldn't want William to break his heart with jealousy. And never a rehearsal, either! The boys were on time to the fraction of a second. It was two hours before a snake could get below Greeley's statue."[9]

"There you are, Kelly, 1,300," said Anthony, tearing off a check. "Your thousand, and the 300 dollars you were out. You don't hate money, do you, Kelly?"

"Me?" said Kelly. "I could lick the man that invented poverty."

Anthony called Kelly when he was at the door. "You didn't notice," he said, "a boy anywhere in the tie-up, did you? A kind of a fat boy without any clothes on shooting arrows around with a bow?"

"Why, no," said Kelly, **mystified**. "I didn't. If he was like you say, maybe the cops grabbed him before I got there."

"I thought the little rascal wouldn't be on hand," chuckled Anthony. "Good-bye, Kelly."

---

7   To *scuttle* a ship is to sink it by cutting holes in its bottom.

8   William A. Brady (1856–1950) was a well-known theater producer.

9   Horace Greeley (1811–1872) was a famous newspaper editor who founded the *New York Tribune*.

## INSIGHTS

In this story, O. Henry indicates that Anthony Rockwall is rich but is not really a member of high society. During the 19th century, a number of men in America started off life with little money, but became very wealthy—often through businesses such as steel and railroads.

Many of these newly rich men had little education but a great deal of business sense. Some of them, like Anthony, valued money over social activities and cultural events. Others, whose families had been rich for several generations, considered themselves better educated, more cultured, and more socially acceptable.

Anthony Rockwall's son Richard has been to college and has developed a taste for both culture and society. But O. Henry clearly thinks the elder Rockwall knows more about the world— and certainly more about what money can or can't buy. Perhaps that's because the author also started off life poor.

O. Henry grew up in the South during a depression that followed the Civil War. At the age of 15, he left school and went to work. It was only after a variety of jobs (and time spent in prison) that he began to sell stories and earn money regularly. But although he identified with self-made, newly rich men, O. Henry managed his own money badly. He was plagued with financial problems for the rest of his life.

# The Gift of the Magi

## VOCABULARY PREVIEW

Below is a list of words that appear in the story. Read the list and get to know the words before you start the story.

**accusation**—a charge of wrongdoing
**adorned**—enhanced the appearance of
**agile**—well-coordinated; quick
**blithely**—merrily; lightheartedly
**calculated**—estimated; figured
**coveted**—wished for enviously; desired
**discreetly**—unnoticeably
**ecstatic**—with overwhelming emotion
**genuine**—authentic; real
**idiocy**—weak-mindedness
**implied**—indirectly expressed; suggested
**laboriously**—requiring much effort
**mammoth**—enormous
**moral**—lesson
**prudence**—caution; foresight
**ransacking**—searching thoroughly
**sequence**—line; row
**truant**—absent without permission; lazy

# The Gift of the Magi

*Although Della had very little money, she was determined to buy her husband a fine Christmas present. She didn't realize that he was working on a similar plan.*

One dollar and 87 cents. That was all. And 60 cents of it was in pennies. They were pennies saved one and two at a time by hard bargaining with the grocer and the vegetable man and the butcher. Her cheeks burned at the silent **accusation** of stinginess that such close dealing **implied**.

Della counted it three times. One dollar and 87 cents. And the next day would be Christmas.

There was clearly nothing to do but flop down on the shabby little couch and howl. So Della did it, which suggests a **moral**— that life is made up of sobs, sniffles, and smiles, with mostly sniffles.

While the mistress of the home is gradually slipping from sobs to sniffles, take a look at the home—a furnished flat[1] at eight dollars per week. It did not exactly beggar description,[2] but it certainly seemed almost suitable for a beggar.

In the lobby below was a letter box into which no letter would go. There was an electric button from which no mortal finger could coax a ring. Also linked with those things was a card bearing the name "Mr. James Dillingham Young."

The "Dillingham" had been **blithely** added during a former period of prosperity. Then its owner was being paid 30 dollars per week.

Now, when the income was shrunk to 20 dollars, the letters

---

1   A *flat* is an apartment that is on one floor of a building.

2   "To beggar description" means to be beyond description.

of "Dillingham" looked blurred. They seemed to be thinking seriously of shrinking to a modest and unassuming *D*.

But whenever Mr. James Dillingham Young came home and reached his flat above, he was called "Jim." And he was greatly hugged by Mrs. James Dillingham Young. She has already been introduced to you as Della, which is all very good.

Della finished her cry and attended to her cheeks with a powder puff. She stood by the window and looked out dully at a gray cat walking a gray fence in a gray backyard. Tomorrow would be Christmas Day. And she had only one dollar and 87 cents with which to buy Jim a present. She had been saving every penny she could for months, with this result.

Twenty dollars a week doesn't go far. Expenses had been greater than she had **calculated**. They always are. Only one dollar and 87 cents to buy a present for Jim—her Jim.

She had spent many a happy hour planning for something nice for him. Something fine and rare and **genuine**. Something almost worthy of the honor of being owned by Jim.

There was a pier glass[3] between the windows of the room. Perhaps you have seen a pier glass in an eight-dollar flat. A very thin person may observe his reflection in a rapid **sequence** of tall strips. A very **agile** person may obtain a fairly accurate idea of his looks. Della, being slender, had mastered the art.

Suddenly she whirled from the window and stood before the glass. Her eyes were shining brilliantly, but her face had lost its color within 20 seconds. Rapidly she pulled down her hair and let it fall to its full length.

Now, there were two possessions of the James Dillingham Youngs in which they both took a great pride. One was Jim's gold watch that had been his father's and his grandfather's. The other was Della's hair.

Had the Queen of Sheba[4] lived in the flat across the air shaft,[5] Della would have shown off her hair. She would have

---

3    A *pier glass* is a tall mirror on the wall between two windows. Those in cheap apartments might be very narrow.

4    Sheba was an ancient Arabian kingdom. In a Biblical story, the Queen of Sheba visited Jerusalem during the rule of King Solomon.

5    An *air shaft* is a vertical opening through the floors of a building. It provides air and some light to inside windows.

let it hang out the window someday to dry, just to ridicule Her Majesty's jewels and gifts.

Had King Solomon[6] been the janitor, Jim would have shown off his watch. Even with treasures piled up in the basement, Jim would have pulled out his watch every time he passed. He would have done it just to see the king pluck at his beard with envy.

So now Della's beautiful hair fell about her, rippling and shining like a cascade of brown waters. It reached below her knee and made itself almost a garment for her. And then she did it up again nervously and quickly. Once she hesitated for a minute and stood still while a tear or two splashed on the worn red carpet.

On went her old brown jacket; on went her old brown hat. With a whirl of skirts, she fluttered out the door and down the stairs to the street. The brilliant sparkle was still in her eyes. Where she stopped, the sign read, "Mme.[7] Sofronie. Hair Goods of All Kinds."

Della ran one flight up and collected herself, panting. Madame was large, too white, and chilly. She hardly looked like a "Sofronie."

"Will you buy my hair?" asked Della.

"I buy hair," said Madame. "Take ye hat off and let's have a sight at the looks of it." Down rippled the brown cascade.

"Twenty dollars," said Madame, lifting the mass with a practiced hand.

"Give it to me quick," said Della.

Oh, and the next two hours tripped by on rosy wings. Forget the hashed metaphor.[8] She was **ransacking** the stores for Jim's present.

She found it at last. It surely had been made for Jim and no one else. There was no other like it in any of the stores, and she had turned all of them inside out. It was a platinum watch chain, simple in design. It properly showed its value by its excellence

6    In the 10th century B.C., King Solomon was the third king of Israel. He was famous for wealth and wisdom.

7    *Mme.* stands for "Madame," a French title equivalent to "Mrs."

8    A *hashed metaphor* is a mixed metaphor. Here the author refers to both walking and flying.

alone, and not by cheap decoration. That is what all good things should do.

It was even worthy of The Watch. As soon as she saw it, she knew that it must be Jim's. It was like him. Quietness and value—the description applied to both. She paid 21 dollars for it, and she hurried home with the 87 cents.

With that chain on his watch, Jim might suitably show an interest in the time in any company. Grand as the watch was, he sometimes looked at it on the sly.[9] That was because of the old leather strap that he used in place of a chain.

When Della reached home, her excitement gave way a little to **prudence** and reason. She got out her curling irons and went to work repairing the damage made by generosity and love. This is always a tremendous task, dear friends—a **mammoth** task.

Within 40 minutes her head was covered with tiny, close-lying curls. They made her look wonderfully like a **truant** schoolboy. She looked at her reflection in the mirror long, carefully, and critically.

"If Jim doesn't kill me," she said to herself, "before he takes a second look at me, he'll say I look like a Coney Island[10] chorus girl. But what could I do? Oh! What could I do with a dollar and 87 cents?"

At 7:00 the coffee was made. The frying pan was on the back of the stove and ready to cook the chops.

Jim was never late. Della doubled up the watch chain in her hand. She sat on the corner of the table near the door that he always entered. Then she heard his step on the stair away down on the first flight. She turned white for just a moment.

Della had a habit of saying little, silent prayers about the simplest everyday things. Now she whispered, "Please, God, make him think I am still pretty."

The door opened, and Jim stepped in and closed it. He looked thin and very serious. Poor fellow, he was only 22 and

---

9   "On the sly" means doing something in a sly or secretive manner.
10  Coney Island—on the Atlantic Ocean in Brooklyn, New York—is a popular tourist resort.

worked hard to support his family. He needed a new overcoat, and he was without gloves.

Jim stopped inside the door, as steady as a setter[11] at the scent of quail. His eyes were fixed upon Della. There was an expression in them that she could not read, and it terrified her. It was not anger, nor surprise, nor disapproval, nor horror. It wasn't any of the emotions that she had been prepared for. He simply stared at her hard, with that peculiar expression on his face.

Della wriggled off the table and went for him.

"Jim, darling," she cried, "don't look at me that way. I had my hair cut off and sold it because I couldn't have lived through Christmas without giving you a present. It'll grow out again. You won't mind, will you? I just had to do it. My hair grows awfully fast. Say 'Merry Christmas!' Jim, and let's be happy. You don't know what a nice—what a beautiful, nice gift I've got for you."

"You've cut off your hair?" asked Jim, **laboriously**. He sounded as if he had not arrived at that obvious fact yet, even after the hardest mental labor.

"Cut it off and sold it," said Della. "Don't you like me just as well, anyhow? I'm me without my hair, ain't I?"

Jim looked around the room curiously.

"You say your hair is gone?" he said, with an air almost of **idiocy**.

"You needn't look for it," said Della. "It's sold, I tell you— sold and gone too. It's Christmas Eve, boy. Be good to me, for it went for you. Maybe the hairs of my head were numbered," she went on with a sudden serious sweetness. "But nobody could ever count my love for you. Shall I put the chops on, Jim?"

Jim seemed to wake quickly out of his trance. He hugged his Della.

For ten seconds let us look **discreetly** at some unimportant object in the other direction. Eight dollars a week or a million a year—what is the difference? A mathematician or a scholar would give you the wrong answer. The magi brought valuable

---

11 A *setter* is a long-haired hunting dog. Setters are trained to crouch and hold their position when game is nearby.

gifts, but the answer to that question was not among them.

Jim drew a package from his overcoat pocket and threw it on the table.

"Don't make any mistake about me, Dell," he said. "I don't think there's anything that could make me like my girl any less. Nothing in the way of a haircut or a shave or a shampoo. But if you'll unwrap that package, you may see why you had me going a while at first."

White and nimble fingers tore at the string and paper. And then an **ecstatic** scream of joy. And then—alas!—a quick change to hysterical tears and wails. This called for the immediate use of all the comforting powers of the lord of the flat.

For there lay The Combs—a set of combs, for side and back. They were the ones that Della had worshipped for so long in a Broadway window. They were beautiful combs, pure tortoise shell with jeweled rims—just the shade to wear in the beautiful vanished hair.

They were expensive combs, she knew. Her heart had simply craved and longed over them without the least hope of owning them. And now they were hers, but the tresses that should have **adorned** the **coveted** adornments were gone.

But she hugged them to her. At last she was able to look up with dim eyes and say, "My hair grows so fast, Jim!"

And then Della leaped up like a little singed cat and cried, "Oh, oh!"

Jim had not yet seen his beautiful present. She held it out to him eagerly in her open palm. The dull precious metal seemed to flash with a reflection of her bright and eager spirit.

"Isn't it a dandy, Jim? I hunted all over town to find it. You'll have to look at the time a hundred times a day now. Give me your watch. I want to see how it looks on it."

Instead of obeying, Jim tumbled down on the couch. He put his hands under the back of his head and smiled.

"Dell," said he, "let's put our Christmas presents away and keep 'em a while. They're too nice to use just now. I sold the watch to get the money to buy your combs. And now suppose you put the chops on."

The magi, as you know, were wise men—wonderfully wise men. They brought gifts to the Babe in the manger.[12] They invented the art of giving Christmas presents. Being wise, their gifts were no doubt wise ones. Possibly they included the privilege of exchange in case of duplication.

And here I have lamely related to you the uneventful story of two foolish children in a flat. They most unwisely sacrificed for each other the greatest treasures of their house. But I have a last word for the wise of these days. Let it be said that of all who give gifts, these two were the wisest.

Of all who give and receive gifts, such as they are the wisest. Everywhere they are the wisest.

They are the magi.

## INSIGHTS

In 1902 O. Henry moved to New York City, and he fell in love with the city and its stories. He was soon writing and selling a story a week for magazines and newspapers. However, when one deadline was approaching, he hadn't even come up with an idea. An editor and an illustrator sat waiting in O. Henry's living room, eager to find out what the illustrator should draw for that week.

Finally the author said, "Just draw a picture of a poorly furnished room . . . on the bed, a man and a girl are sitting side by side. They're talking about Christmas. The man has a watch fob[13] in his hand. The girl's principal feature is her long, beautiful hair  . . . That's all I can think of now, but the story is coming."

"The Gift of the Magi" turned out to be one of O. Henry's most popular stories. It features the kind of ironic twist at the end that he so often used. And the public loved these "surprise" endings. In 1906 the story was published again, in a collection of O. Henry's New York stories called *The Four Million.*

---

12  *The Babe* refers to the baby Jesus, the son of God.

13  A *watch fob* is a short chain or ribbon attached to a pocket watch.